GOOD CENTS

every kid's guide to making money

by members of
The Amazing Life Games Company
(and friends)
illustrated by Martha Hairston
and James Robertson

Houghton Mifflin Company Boston
1974

Library of Congress Cataloging in Publication Data

Amazing Life Games Company.
    Good cents.

    SUMMARY: A collection of schemes that suggest how
to make money and what to do with it (besides spend it).
    1. Self-employed--Juvenile literature. 2. Small
business--Juvenile literature. 3. Finance, Personel--
Juvenile literature. [1. Business. 2. Finance,
Personal] I. Title.
HD8036.A45 1974   658'.022   74-9378
ISBN 0-395-19500-4
ISBN 0-395-19501-2 (pbk.)

This book was edited and prepared for publication
at The Yolla Bolly Press in Sausalito, California,
during the months of February to June 1974.

We would like to say that we have written this book
in a way that we think kids will understand most easily.
In places, we have taken liberties with traditional rules
of grammar and style, but have done this with the goal
of making it easier for our readers to negotiate the
material.—*The Editors.*

Printed in the United States of America.

First Printing H G

About This Book

If you just want to have fun, read some other book. This one is about having fun (and making money) by doing work. Hard work. You can't have one without the other.

Remember this: you'll have to do some serious thinking on your own. No book can tell you what's right for you. Any book that says different is a liar.

This book is also about caring. You can't have much fun if you don't care about the things you do.

Everybody is good at something. *Everybody.* And usually (but not always) people like to do what they are good at. It makes them feel right inside. It's important to try to figure out what you're good at.

A lot of the ideas adults have about money and work are pretty crazy. Don't be fooled. Especially don't pay much attention to people who think that making a lot of money is equal to being happy. They are the craziest of all. The next craziest are those people who spend all day doing something they hate. The ones who say, "I'm not good at anything," aren't crazy, they're just sad.

This book was made by a bunch of grownups. But we couldn't have done it without the help of a lot of kids. Some kids sent us stories about their work. Other kids made things, tried out the ideas, did drawings or told us when they thought an idea was too corny. We thank them very much. And we all hope you like this book.

Tanya Broder
Dana Konopaski
Berit
Ingo
Adrienne Brayman
Lael Robertson
Keila Diehl
Nicholas Wale
Jacqueline White

Bart Haines
Jon Wilson
Toby Wilson
Martha P. Hairston
Marjorie Winter
Sadako McInerney
Queenie Minion Taylor
Carolyn Robertson
Jamie Jolt
JAMES ROBERTSON

What's In This Book

Weekenders

Any Timers

Special Timers

Weekenders

THE SATURDAY & SUNDAY STUFF & JUNK COMPANY

What can you do with bottle caps? Or tin cans? What kind of nifty thing could you make out of old newspapers? How could you make an old tee shirt, torn bed sheet, or holey bath towel into something useful? Some of the best ideas for things to do (and make money) come from the junk heap. If you think about it for a while, you'll think of your own ideas. But while you're thinking, here are some ideas we know about that you could try. Once you get going, you can make a good after school or Saturday business out of making miracles out of junk and other stuff, and selling them in your neighborhood.

Tin Can Jangles

A simple device that you make from the lids of small tin cans and some strong string. They look nice (after you get done painting them). They sound nice in a breeze. And if you have a garden, they'll discourage the birds from eating seeds or plants before they can grow up into vegetables and flowers.

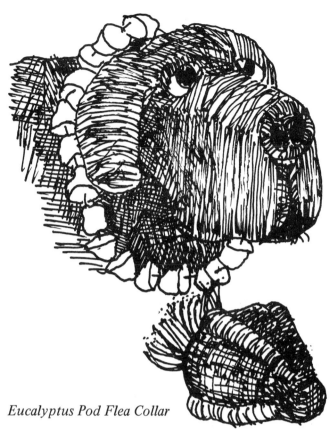

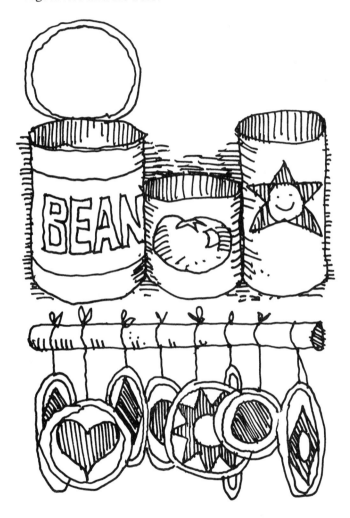

You'll need: A bunch of tin cans (tomato paste size up to soup or canned peaches size). A file for smoothing out the edges so they don't cut fingers. A good can opener. Some enamel paint and brushes. String and sticks for the tops.

Collect lids and bottoms (or cut them out with the can opener).

Eucalyptus Pod Flea Collar

If you live where eucalyptus trees grow, you can make organic flea collars for dogs and cats. Fleas do not like the smell of eucalyptus pods. Dogs and people don't mind it at all. So instead of putting a collar full of poison around the dog's neck, your customers could use a collar that smells nice and won't hurt anyone but the fleas.

What You Need: A eucalyptus tree that is making pods. They are best when they're green with fuzzy beards. The smell lasts longest then. But they'll work even later when they turn dark and get hard. Something sharp to make holes through them. (An ice pick would be good.) String and a strong needle with a big eye.

String the pods on a length of heavy string. (Do not use wire.) Tie the ends securely with a bow. That's so your customer can adjust the necklace later to the size of the dog's neck. It's a good idea to make a little tag that tells about the collar. Sell them for $1 each.

Bottle Cap Door Mat

If you can collect enough of them, bottle caps make a good door mat. It takes about 300 of them to make a mat about 16 by 20 inches. The best place to get caps is anywhere there is a soft drink machine. Any kind of cap works, even the twist-off kind.

Get a board about 16 by 20 inches. Plywood is the best if it is exterior-type plywood, the kind that withstands water. It should be at least 5/8 of an inch thick. Drive a nail in the middle of each cap. Make rows with the caps just touching each other. After the caps are all nailed in place, you could paint the mat with a spray can. This kind of mat is perfect for scraping the mud off dirty boots or shoes.

Sell each mat for $2 or more.

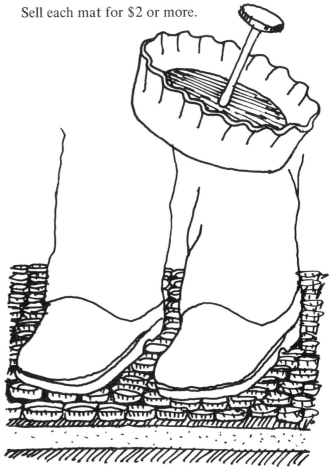

Liver Lids

You can make these anywhere you can collect the plastic lids that come on the top of plastic containers that liver or sometimes chicken parts come in at the meat counter. You can tell the lids because they are quite clear, and have little colored lines around the edges. You'll need lids and magic markers and an oven.

First, draw a design on the plastic lid with the markers. You can draw on one side or both.

Then pop the lid into the oven. Set the temperature at about 450 degrees. After it has been in there for a minute or so, take a peek and see the magic. The lid has shrunk into a tiny plastic disc, and with it, your drawing. Press the disc flat with a pancake turner while it is still hot.

If you punch a hole in the edge with a paper punch *before* you cook them, your liver lids can be hung up on a string. They look beautiful!

Sell them for 25 cents each.

the broom handle. Squeeze the water out as you roll. Add a second layer the same way. Then gently remove the broom handle and let the logs dry thoroughly. (It will take several days unless they are in a warm dry place.)

The broomstick helps you make the log by giving you something to roll the paper around. But it also does something else that is important. When the log burns, the hole helps the heat to reach the center of the log and burn it all the way through. The detergent is used to make the log sticky enough so that the paper stays stuck in the log shape, even after it's dry.

How Much To Charge. That depends partly on you and partly on your customers. Make the price as low as you can. People will probably pay 10 cents a log. Maybe more if they can't get firewood at a reasonable price.

Newspaper Logs

Everyone has old newspapers. A lot of people have fireplaces, and firewood is very expensive to buy. But you can make fireplace logs out of old newspapers that will burn almost as long as a pine log the same size. And unless there is an awful lot of free firewood around, people will buy them.

What You Need. Lots of old newspapers. A big tub. A broom handle or a dowel about that size. Some detergent. A good place to dry them.

How To Make Logs. First make some samples and try them out in your own fireplace, or get a neighbor to try them. See how long they burn. Make some bigger and some smaller and see which works best. To begin with, try this:

Soak some folded newspapers (a stack about an inch thick) in the tub containing water and detergent. Let the papers soak all the way through. Take them out and roll them around

13

saturday laundromat express

Next time you're out, look in the window of the laundromat. You'll have to look hard to find a more unhappy-looking bunch of people. No one likes to sit around waiting for the washer to finish so they can put their stuff in the dryer. Or wait for the dryer to finish so they can fold it all and schlep it home. It's hot. There is nothing to do. Everyone is miserable.

But you can make it pleasant, and at the same time make yourself a job. The first thing to do is to find a laundromat manager who is willing to let you help him. He can't be there all the time. (He might run several places and just come around when the machines break down.) You aren't asking him for money. You are offering a service to his customers that will make his laundromat better. Tell him exactly what you'll do. And tell him if you don't make his customers happy, you'll stop. That's a good deal and if he doesn't go for it, he's crazy and you should find someone else. Here's what you do:

NEW EXTRA SERVICE

MY NAME IS MARTHA. I'M HERE EVERY SATURDAY MORNING. I WILL WAIT FOR YOUR CLOTHES WHILE YOU SHOP. I WILL DRY THEM AND FOLD THEM FOR ONLY 25¢. I WILL DELIVER TO YOUR HOUSE FOR 25¢ EXTRA.

1. Make two signs like the one shown below. Put one sign in the window and the other inside on a table or where you wait for business. Be sure the signs are big and easy to read. Put drawings on them.

2. Bring some magazines. Bring comics for kids and National Geographic and Time and Good Housekeeping and Woman's Day for grownups. Also bring Sports Illustrated and the daily paper. The magazines can be old, but the paper should be current. Keep these at your table. Offer them to customers. Then ask them if you can help them with their laundry.

3. When you take an order, write down the customer's name and address and phone so you will know how to contact them if you need to. This will also help you keep track of orders when you're busy. If you are very busy, you'll have to hire a friend to help with the deliveries. You don't want to miss customers while you're out delivering.

4. Be sure to be there regularly. If you appear each Saturday (or whenever you say you will), people will get to know you. They will see that you do a good job and that you can be counted on. Then they will depend on you. So be there on time. And always do what you say you will. That's an important part of any service.

5. How much you can make depends on how busy the laundromat is. Once people know you, it should be easy to handle a dozen orders on a busy morning. That's $3.00.

You know how your parents like to sleep late on Sundays? Well, most people are like that. They also like to read the paper and take it easy. If you're willing to get up early, you can make lots of people happy by bringing the Sunday morning paper to them. It's better than a paper route because you only work one morning a week. Here's how it works:

Make the rounds in your apartment building or neighborhood. Ask everyone who doesn't subscribe to a paper if they would like you to bring it to them on Sunday. Lots of people don't get a paper delivered every day. They have to go to the newsstand. Tell them you charge for the paper plus 25¢ for delivery. Ask them what time they want you to bring it. Write down each order, including the time.

Or you could make a notice like this to slip under the doors in your apartment building.

Then make arrangements with a newsstand to get the papers either early Sunday or late Saturday. You pay for the papers when you pick them up. Then you sell them to your customers and keep the money.

How much you make depends on the number of customers you get. In a city it should be pretty easy to get at least ten customers. That's $2.50 each Sunday morning.

My name is Irving. I live in APT 4C. I will bring you a sunday morning paper each weekend if you want. I charge for the paper plus 25¢ for delivery. Put your name here and return this order. If you want my service. PS I'm saving for season tickets to the METS.

name _____ apt _____
I WANT MY PAPER AT _____ OCLOCK

The Sunday Paper Delux

Once you get newspaper customers, you can add to your service. Make arrangements with a bakery to pick up hot Danish or bagels early Sunday morning. Then offer hot breakfast pastry with your Sunday morning paper. Charge an extra 25¢ plus the cost of the pastry.

THE USED MUSIC COMPANY AND RECORD EXCHANGE

Here is a good way you can turn old records that no one wants into a dandy once-in-a-while business. Everyone who has a record player has old records they never listen to. And most people will be happy to have you take them away for nothing. You'll get old children's records that you or other kids have outgrown, or old 45 rpm records that were popular three years ago, or old long playing albums that aren't needed. Classical, popular, rock, jazz, or western. All kinds.

MAKE THE ROUNDS OF YOUR NEIGHBOR-HOOD TO COLLECT THE RECORDS. TELL EVERONE WHO GIVES YOU RECORDS TO COME TO YOUR BIG SALE. TELL THEM THAT IF THEY DON'T WANT TO GIVE YOU RECORDS, THEY CAN COME AND TRADE.

PICK A SATURDAY MORNING OR AFTER-NOON FOR YOUR SALE AND BE SURE TO ADVERTISE BEFORE.
YOU COULD MAKE POSTERS LIKE THIS TO PUT AROUND YOUR NEIGH-BORHOOD :

OR HAVE A PARADE WITH SIGNS.

You could make tickets and give them away free to tell people when and where the big sale is.

On the day of your sale, get a big table and put all the records out in boxes. Try dividing them into kinds (kids', classical, etc.). Have a record player or radio there so people can hear music while they buy. (It will also attract customers.) List your big hits on a poster or blackboard.

Sell 45s for 15 cents
    78s for 25 cents
    33s (albums) for 50 cents

If someone has a record to trade, then they should get any record for only a dime, plus their record in trade. If you have lots of records, you could make special prices for people buying more than one of a kind (two 45s for 25 cents).

Be sure to put your sale in a place where people will see it. A garage right near the sidewalk is a good place. And to make your sale hard to resist, make a big huge bowl of free popcorn and sell little cups of apple juice for 5 cents. There is nothing like popcorn, apple juice and used music for attracting a crowd.

Pay attention to the musicians that people seem most interested in. Then the next time you have a Used Music Sale, you'll know who to put at the top of your list.

WRAPPING UP

MAKE JACKETS FOR THE RECORDS THAT DON'T HAVE THEM OUT OF WRAPPING PAPER PIECES OR PAPER BAG SIDES. DECORATE WITH CRAYONS OR MARKERS. CUT HOLES IN EACH SIDE OF THE JACKET SO THE RECORD TITLES SHOW THROUGH.

CUSTOMER PLUS
IF YOU CAN GET YOUR HANDS ON ANY OLD FAN MAGAZINES SELL THOSE TOO. GROWNUPS GET A CHARGE OUT OF SEEING PICTURES OF RECORDING STARS THAT WERE THEIR TEENAGE FAVORITES.

Here's a small list of recording artists to be on the look-out for in getting together your **BIG HITS** list.

Teenagers might like:

Beatles	Black Sabbath
Rolling Stones	Led Zeppelin
The Who	Osmond Brothers
Jackson Five	David Cassidy

Parents might like:

Beach Boys	Elvis Presley
Bob Dylan	Temptations
Lovin' Spoonful	Miracles

Grandparents might like:

Ella Fitzgerald	Nat "King" Cole
Dave Brubeck	Woody Herman
Benny Goodman	Henry Mancini

If you were a dog, your idea of heaven would probably be to be outdoors sniffing the air, the trees, the grass, or playing fetch, or having your ears or your belly scratched, or that place on your back just where your tail starts—that place you can't scratch by yourself. Well, gang, if you live in a city and like dogs, you can do your dog friends, your human neighbors and yourself a bit of good work by starting a really good dog walking service.

Hey Bingo! Wanna go for a walk?

A really good dog walking service is very simple. There are two most important parts to it. It is always there on time, and it is polite to the human customers. To the dog customers, it always knows how to be a good friend, and at the same time makes sure no dog gets into trouble.

Advertise. To get your first customers, pick an apartment building, or some other place where people have dogs with no yard. Try to find people who work all week and need their weekends to do other things. They are the ones who need your service the most.

Start small. You've probably seen those professional dog walkers in big cities. They have lots of dogs on leashes. They stagger around and no one has any fun. Dogs are smart animals. They know better. Treat each dog like the intelligent animal he or she is. Each is different. See what they like best. Try to make the walk the most fun you can. Never take more than two dogs at a time. And at first, don't take more than one.

Find dog places. *Dogs get bored like anyone else. And nothing is as boring to a dog as being indoors all the time. So when you take dogs outside, take them to dog places. Places with grass. Empty lots. The spaces behind buildings, or under bridges. Parks where there are people and children. Playgrounds.*

Know how to avoid trouble. *Start by knowing what your dogs can and can't do. Most cities have passed ordinances that make it unlawful for dogs to use sidewalks as bathrooms. Some cities don't want dogs in parks. Some have leash laws. Find out about these things and pay attention to them. Remember that each owner is trusting you with a member of their family. That's a big responsibility. Never go off, even for a minute, and leave dogs alone, even if you tie them up.*

Use short leashes. *Bring along your own leash. The short kind is best because it is easier to hold and won't tangle. And you can let go and let the dog run without having to take it off.*

Give yourself a break. *If you charge $1 for fifty minutes, that means you get a ten minute rest each hour. You could do four dogs in a morning. That means $4, or more if you can take two dogs at once. And that's pretty good pay for half a Saturday. Give yourself at least ten minutes to rest between dogs. You'll need it.*

Here is a treat for your dog. On **Saturdays** I can treat you too by taking your dog for a **50 minute** healthy walk for exercise and fun. ($1.00) Make a reservation for your dog. Call any afternoon after school or evening. My name is Donald Segretti. My phone number is MU8-6845

Presenting: THE BEST BABYSITTERS EVER!

This is a way you can turn an old idea into a brand new business and make work that might be boring into something enjoyable for everyone. Most kids do babysitting at some time or other. Well, if you can do babysitting, you can certainly start a Weekend Babysitters Co-op. What's that? That's where you and a friend invite mothers or dads you know to leave their children at your house on Saturday mornings or afternoons while they go shopping, or to the football game, and so forth. And instead of just sitting, you organize games and projects for the kids and have a fine old time. Here's how:

First, get together with a friend and plan how your co-op will work. You'll need to know when you want to do it, who's house it'll be in, what activities to plan for the kids, and who to tell about it.

Let's start a babysitting co-op.

O.K!

We need to decide how much to charge, so how about 50¢ an hour for each kid?

What if we do it next Saturday? That's a football day, so we could start at noon.

Babysitting Special!! SAT. NOV. 18 12-5 p.m. Going to the GAME? Bring your kids to our co-op first! Frank Hill Julie Kay 225 Oakdale Av.

8100 WILSONS

Let people know about your service at least a week in advance. Start by calling your regular customers or going to see them. You could also put notices in their mail boxes. Have people call you ahead of time so you'll know how many kids to plan for.

20

ON THE BIG DAY...

HAVE ONE ROOM SET UP TO HAVE YOUR COOP IN, LIKE A FAMILY ROOM OR BASEMENT. HAVE A PLACE TO PUT THEIR COATS AND BOOTS.

ACTIVITIES

Here're some ideas for activities you could do. Remember to plan ahead so you'll have the things you need. Use stuff you have around the house— old crayons and chalk, newspapers and paper bags—and keep what you buy to a minimum so you don't spend more than you make.

PAINT A GROUP PORTRAIT. DO IT ON PAPER BAGS CUT OPEN, TAPED TOGETHER ON THE BACK AND THEN TAPED TO A WALL. IF YOU USE PAINTS, BE SURE TO PROVIDE OLD SHIRTS FOR SMOCKS.

HELP THE KIDS MAKE GIFTS FOR THEIR PARENTS....CARDS, PICTURES, TIN·CAN PENCIL HOLDERS.....

HAVE EXTRA THINGS AROUND FOR KIDS TO PLAY WITH IF THEY DON'T WANT TO BE PART OF THE GROUP......CRAYONS, PAPER, TOYS, PUZZLES, ETC.....

Have A Talent Show—or a costume parade, or a skit. Let the kids dress up in old clothes you provide and do their own show, either for you or the returning grownups. You might help by suggesting a story or characters.

Pick A Theme—like Autumn, maybe, if it's September. Go for a walk and collect pretty leaves. Or have the kids cut colored paper into leaf shapes and use them to decorate the room for a cookies and juice party later.

Make Cookies. This is a big project and you should be sure to have all the ingredients and lots of space to work in before you start.

Your Theme Could Be *Animals.* You could read some animal stories. The kids could make paper bag masks and give an animal play; make animal shaped cookies; draw pictures of their favorite animals or cut them out of magazines and glue them onto paper.

Pick out a simple sugar cookie recipe that you've made before. Let the kids help with stirring, shaping and decorating the cookies. Decorate them with food coloring (a few drops added to the batter or on each cookie) or raisins, nuts, candies, chocolate chips or jam.

IF PEOPLE BRING BABIES OR CRAWLERS, YOU'LL NEED SOMEONE TO TAKE CARE OF THEM — MAYBE EACH OF YOU COULD TAKE TURNS OR, IF LOTS OF KIDS ARE COMING, GET A THIRD FRIEND TO HELP.

GET A PLAY PEN TO HELP WITH THE CRAWLERS.

PLAN A QUIET TIME FOR ALL THE KIDS AND FOR YOU. (MAYBE YOU COULD HAVE A SPECIAL QUIET ROOM FOR THE BABIES' NAPS.) TRY TO HAVE 15 OR 20 MINUTES WHEN EVERYONE LIES DOWN TO REST OR DO A QUIET THING, LIKE LOOK AT PICTURE BOOKS.

AND DON'T FORGET....
① HAVE A FIRST AID KIT AROUND TO TAKE CARE OF SMALL ACCIDENTS.
② TRY TO HAVE MORE THAN ENOUGH ACTIVITIES PLANNED. AFTER YOU HAVE DONE A FEW OF THESE YOU'LL HAVE A BETTER IDEA OF HOW LONG THINGS WILL TAKE TO DO.

③ AFTER YOU'VE HAD A COUPLE OF CO-OP DAYS FOR PEOPLE YOU KNOW, ADVERTISE WITH LITTLE POSTERS ON BULLETIN BOARDS IN LAUNDROMATS, OR GROCERY STORES. ④ BE SURE TO KEEP TRACK OF HOW LONG EACH KID STAYS SO YOU'LL KNOW HOW MUCH TO CHARGE THEIR PARENTS.

Jacqueline White has a paper route in reverse. She lives in Milwaukee, Wisconsin, and believes that people need trees just as much as they need newspapers. She has arranged to collect papers from people in her neighborhood on a regular schedule, and then turns them in to a collection center which ships them back to be made into more newsprint. It's a pretty good idea and it's one of the ways Jacqueline earns money. Just like a paper route—only backwards.

Here is how you could do it:

First check around to be sure that there is a place near you which will purchase used newspaper. (See what other kind of paper they will buy, too. Some will pay for magazines and corrugated cardboard; others won't.) In Jacqueline's area, $1 is paid for every 100 pounds.

Then make up a little advertisement to take around to all the houses in your neighborhood. Say something like this:

> PLEASE HELP ME SAVE TREES
> 🌲🌲🌲
> I HAVE A BACKWARDS PAPER ROUTE.
> ONCE EACH 2 WEEKS I WILL COLLECT ALL
> YOUR OLD PAPERS AND TAKE THEM TO A
> PLACE THAT MAKES THEM INTO NEW
> PAPER. CALL SANDRA IF YOU WANT
> THIS SERVICE. MY PHONE IS TU 4-1058

This is a picture of Jacqueline taken by her father on one of their trips to the paper collection center near them. Look in the Yellow Pages of your phone book under "Waste Paper" for the names of companies that buy used paper.

If you provide the service of stacking and tying the bundles, too, you should probably charge 5 cents a bundle for getting them ready. Most of your customers will be willing to pay you to do that for them. Be sure to use good strong twine (not string) for your bundles so they won't come apart. Collect the bundles in a wagon and stack them in your garage, or wherever there is room out of the rain. When you have collected 500 pounds or so, ask a grownup friend to help you take them to the collection center.

THE FOOTBALL APPLE SHINERS

Did you know that football games and apple trees go together? They do. Because football games and apples happen at about the same time of year. And if you live in a place where there are some of both, you're in luck. You can have a Saturday afternoon business selling your home-shined, fresh picked apples at the football game.

(This is also a way to please your little brother or sister who is too little to do work all alone. You could make him or her your partner.)

First you need to collect apples. Find a person with lots of apples and tell them that you will mow their lawn (or clean up their yard, or wash their car, etc.) if they'll let you pick a wagon full of apples from their tree. Get a couple of strong wooden boxes to put the apples in.

Next, sort the apples. Put the beauties in one pile (gently) and the not-so-glamorous ones in another pile. Then wash all of them in clean water and polish them with a soft cloth. Make them good and shiny.

Super Good Apples
10¢ or
5¢
each

Paint your boxes with bright colors and make a sign to put on your wagon. Sell the beauties for a dime each and the others for a nickle. Get there early and don't be afraid to shout, so people know you're there. Or take along a noise-maker. Here are some noise-makers:

You might even get in the gate and see the game for free!

THE CLEARVIEW WINDOW WASHERS...

This is an idea that will work if you live in a neighborhood with houses. If you live in a neighborhood with twenty story apartment buildings, it will probably not work, and you better look for another idea.

This idea is based on the fact that most grownups do not like to clean dirty windows. It's not hard work. It's just a lot of bother. A few people *do* like to clean windows. If you are one of those people, then you can probably spend as much time as you want making windows clean for people and getting paid for it.

WHAT YOU'LL NEED:
A LADDER
SOME WINDOW CLEANER
SOME NEWSPAPERS OR
NON-LINTY RAGS
AND MAYBE A
SQUEEGEE AND
SPONGE AND A
BUCKET

A BIG JAR OF WINDEX OR SOME OTHER COMMERCIAL WINDOW SPRAY COSTS 79¢.
YOU CAN MAKE YOUR OWN IF YOU WANT. JUST MIX ONE TABLESPOON OF MR. CLEAN IN ½ A PAIL OF WARM WATER.

WHERE TO LOOK FOR BUSINESS

STEP LADDERS ARE EXPENSIVE SO BORROW ONE IF YOU CAN. THE KIND WITH A LITTLE SHELF FOR YOUR RAGS AND CLEANER WORKS BEST.

IF YOU USE WINDEX WIPE IT OFF WITH SMALL FOLDED SHEETS OF NEWSPAPER OR RAGS. BE SURE TO ASK YOUR MOM FOR RAGS THAT WON'T LEAVE A LOT OF LINT (FUZZ) ON THE GLASS.

MOST PROFESSIONALS DON'T USE SPRAY CLEANERS, THEY USE WATER (OR LIQUID CLEANER LIKE THE KIND YOU MAKE YOURSELF.) THEY PUT IT ON WITH A SPONGE, LIKE ①, AND TAKE IT OFF WITH A RUBBER SQUEEGEE, LIKE ②, WHICH ALSO DRIES THE WINDOW. YOU CAN GET ONE FOR $3.00.

One nice thing about this business is that you can see who needs you. Just look around. But be tactful. Some people don't like to be told that you see they have dirty windows. Say it politely.

Tell your mother's friends. (And your friends' mothers.) Tell your neighbors. If you are acquainted with people who own stores in your neighborhoods, tell them too.

Make a little notice that you can give people with your name and phone number. Take it to all the real estate agents. Tell them you think people who come to look at houses to buy like to see clean windows. (That one works!)

WINDOW WASHERS
Good Rates!
Good Workers!
Good Results!
Call Harold
77...
...21

How To Charge For Your Service

You should keep your prices as reasonable as you can. That will encourage people to have you do their windows often. There are two ways to charge: by the window, or by the hour. By the window you could charge 50 cents for medium sized ones, a dime extra if they have lots of little panes. Charge more for great big windows, less for little ones. By the hour, charge $1.50 to $2.50, depending on how experienced you are. If you work fast and don't leave spots, charge more. At first, charge a little less, until you get good at it.

SPECIAL HINTS

DON'T DO ANY WINDOWS THAT ARE ABOVE THE FIRST FLOOR LEVEL. IT IS TOO DANGEROUS. STAY ON THE GROUND.

NEVER LEAN YOUR LADDER AGAINST THE GLASS, ONLY ON THE WALL, OR ON THE FRAME. NO ONE WILL ASK YOU BACK IF YOU BREAK A WINDOW THE FIRST TIME.

CLEAN BOTH SIDES OF EACH WINDOW. IF YOU HAVE TO GO INSIDE TO DO IT, BE VERY CAREFUL NOT TO SPILL CLEANER INDOORS.

WORK QUICKLY BUT DO A GOOD JOB.

CLEAN WINDOWS MAKE EVERYONE CHEERFUL. CHECK YOUR WORK CAREFULLY TO MAKE SURE YOU LEAVE NO STREAKS AND YOU'LL ALWAYS HAVE HAPPY CUSTOMERS.

BEFORE YOU LEAVE, ASK EACH CUSTOMER TO CHECK YOUR WORK TO BE SURE YOU HAVEN'T FORGOTTEN A WINDOW.

KEEP A NOTEBOOK WITH THE NAMES AND ADDRESSES OF YOUR CUSTOMERS AND THE DATE YOU LAST CLEANED THEIR WINDOWS. AFTER THREE OR FOUR MONTHS HAVE GONE BY, GO BACK AND ASK THEM IF THEY WOULD LIKE YOU TO COME BACK. BET THEY'LL SAY YES.

Summer is the perfect time to start your own Dog Wash Service. Just think how many dogs you could wash if you and four of your friends set up a super-dooper dog wash production line in your backyard. Just think how many clean dogs and happy owners there would be.

What You'll Need

leashes (or rope)
two large shallow plastic or galvanized metal tubs
a hose and lots of water
dog shampoo or a mild soap
old towels or rags
dog biscuits (for rewards)

This is how it might look:

1 The manager/dog handler

2 The washer

3 The rinser

4 The dryer

5 The goodie giver

How To Advertise

Make some eye-catching posters with time, date and price. Hang them in your local vet's office, pet store or laundromat. You can go around your neighborhood and tell your neighbors about your service. You might even get some appointments in advance. Charge $1 per wash. You could make this into a regular service once every other week if you have lots of dogs in your neighborhood. You might be able to wash ten dogs in one afternoon. Be sure to wear old clothes.

Recycling is hard work, but it can be fun if you and some of your friends are really concerned about saving our earth's resources. If you believe in saving trees and if you think junk yards have too much good junk that shouldn't be wasted but used again, then this job is for you. You'll earn some money, but the most important reward may be the satisfaction of knowing that you are doing something to help stop the waste of earth's resources.

Before you start on your new business, you will need to find out:

1. Is there a recycling center in your town or a town nearby? If so, you are in luck. Tell them you plan to be the manager of a recycling depot in your neighborhood. Make a deal with them to pick up your stuff when you get a truckload-full, or to help you find another way to deliver the stuff.

2. If there isn't a center in your town, then ask your father, mother, big brother, or a grownup friend to help you. The biggest problem will be moving the tin, glass, newspaper and aluminum from your neighborhood to a place where it will be processed to be used again. Hopefully, a grownup will share your enthusiasm for this idea. If so, you are ready to get started.

How To Set Up Your Depot

Set up your depot in your garage, backyard or a vacant lot. (Get the owner's permission first.) You will need at least five large garbage cans or oil drums. Label them like this: <u>tin cans, aluminum cans, green glass, white glass, brown glass.</u> It is very important that each item be correctly prepared and sorted for recycling. Here's the way to prepare:

Tin cans: Remove tops, bottoms and the paper wrapper. The next step is to stomp the cans flat. Play music while you do this because it's more fun that way.

Bottles: Must be clean and free of metal caps. It is important to separate the glass by color. The next step could be dangerous if you aren't careful: the glass should be broken so it takes less space. This is usually done by putting the bottles whole in the metal garbage can and smashing them with a heavy pipe. Wear protective glasses and gloves. Be sure no one comes near while you're working.

Aluminum: Cans must be all-aluminum and not bi-metal. You can identify bi-metal cans by the seam that runs up the side. Aluminum cans are seamless and they are very easy to crush, even with your bare hands.

Newspapers: Should be neatly stacked and tied both ways with heavy string.

Cardboard: Boxes should be flattened and stacked. Tie them, too.

Set a time—like every Saturday from 10 am to 3 pm—for receiving items. Prepare a flyer to circulate around your neighborhood. Briefly explain how each item should be prepared so people will learn how to clean, sort and crush these items at home. If people bring you cans not crushed, tell them you will do it but you charge 75 cents a box-full. Most people will do it themselves once they get into the habit. When your garage or back yard gets real full and you think you've reached the limits of your space, it's time to call your grownup to help you deliver your items to your town's recycling center or to the various factories that accept these items for re-use.

The prices for recycled items in our town are:

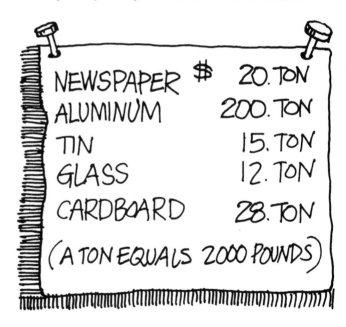

NEWSPAPER $ 20. TON
ALUMINUM 200. TON
TIN 15. TON
GLASS 12. TON
CARDBOARD 28. TON
(A TON EQUALS 2000 POUNDS)

There might be other ways you could earn more money. But we don't know any way you could earn any money and feel better about your work. A neighborhood recycling depot is one of the best ways we know to help everyone.

31

THE GOPHER ERRAND SERVICE

When you run errands, you're a gopher. You go fer groceries. You go fer the newspaper. You go fer something at the drug store or bakery. 'Course if you're not fond of gophers, you could call your service "The Greased Lightning Errand Service," or "The Speeding Bullet Errand Service," or whatever you like.

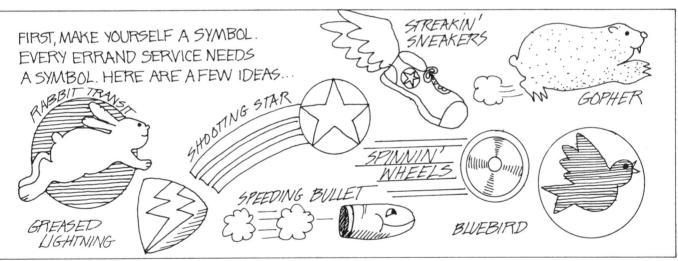

FIRST, MAKE YOURSELF A SYMBOL. EVERY ERRAND SERVICE NEEDS A SYMBOL. HERE ARE A FEW IDEAS...

RABBIT TRANSIT

STREAKIN' SNEAKERS

GOPHER

SHOOTING STAR

SPINNIN' WHEELS

SPEEDING BULLET

GREASED LIGHTNING

BLUEBIRD

Next make little announcements you can take around town. Give them to friends. Post them on bulletin boards at the supermarket. They might say something like this: ———→

Be sure to put your symbol on the poster. (You could also put it on your bike and on a tee shirt if you don't think that's too corny.)

THE RAIN OR SHINE ERRAND SERVICE

The next time you forget something at the store, don't drive back for it. CALL GRETCHEN HUMPHREY I will get it for you on my bike. Anything that will fit in my basket can be delivered to your door in a few minutes. Call 774 4546 any afternoon, 3-5 or Saturdays, 10-5.

HOW TO CHARGE

TRY TO KEEP YOUR FEES SMALL.
25¢ TO 50¢ FOR SHORT TRIPS. 50¢ TO $1.00
FOR LONG ONES OR TWO TRIPS. HERE
IS AN EXAMPLE:
MRS FINDLEY CALLS AND TELLS YOU THAT SHE'D
LIKE YOU TO GO TO THE PET STORE AND GET
HER A POUND OF LIVER FOR HER CAT.

WHAT TO CHARGE

① FIRST YOU HAVE TO GO TO MRS FINDLEY'S PLACE TO PICK UP THE MONEY.

  **25¢**

② THEN YOU HAVE TO GO TO THE STORE AND BUY THE LIVER.

③ FINALLY, YOU BRING IT BACK TO MRS FINDLEY.

 **25¢**

IF MRS. FINDLEY LIVES A LONG WAY FROM YOU, AND THE PET STORE IS A LONG WAY FROM MRS FINDLEY, THEN YOU SHOULD CHARGE MORE FOR EACH TRIP.

TOTAL: 50¢

---

1. Be dependable. That means if you advertise that your service is available every day, then you have to do it every day. So start with Saturdays only. Or just a couple of afternoons (the same ones) each week.

2. Think about what kind of people need your service most. People who don't have cars. People who sell small things that you can carry easily. Old people who have trouble getting out regularly. Be sure you've thought about who these people are and where they are, first. Then be sure they know about you.

3. Be patient. It will take time for people to learn about your new service. Then it will take a while for them to learn they can count on you. You'll have to advertise regularly at first. But pretty soon, you'll get regular customers.

4. Once you've tried the business for a while, go to the drug store and tell the druggist that you would like to deliver for him too. Try the same thing with other stores.

The White Tornado Basement Cleaners and Garage Sale Company

"Gunk" for greasy floors

IS YOUR GARAGE FULL OF JUNK? The White Tornado Company can help!!

We clean basements & garages. Free estimates

Call Katy - 452-8821 or RON - 452-8643 !GOOD RATES!

Liquid soap

trash bags
cardboard boxes

old clothes

stepladder sponges buckets mop wagon rags scrub brush

THIS IS TWO IDEAS IN ONE. FIRST: CLEANING BASEMENTS OR GARAGES AND HAULING AWAY JUNK. SECOND: SELLING JUNK YOU HAUL AWAY FROM THE PLACES YOU CLEAN. TRY IT AS A WEEKEND BUSINESS. CLEAN BASEMENTS ON SATURDAYS UNTIL YOU HAVE GATHERED ENOUGH GOOD JUNK TO SELL. THEN HAVE A GIANT GARAGE OR BASEMENT SALE THE NEXT SATURDAY. YOU CAN MAKE MONEY BOTH WAYS.

IDEA NUMBER **1**: CLEANING BASEMENTS AND GARAGES

First make a list of everyone you and your friends can think of who has a basement or garage or attic that might need a good cleaning. Then make signs or notices that tell about your business. Put them where people will see them. When someone calls you up, be sure to tell them how many workers you will bring, what cleaning materials you can bring and what tools or materials your customer may have to provide.

DOING JOBS

① ARRIVE ON TIME AND READY TO WORK. TELL THE CUSTOMER HOW MUCH YOU WILL CHARGE FOR THE JOB. CHARGE $3.00 FOR A SMALL JOB, $4.00 OR $5.00 FOR A LARGE ONE. (PRACTICE ON YOUR OWN BASEMENT FIRST SO YOU'LL KNOW HOW LONG A JOB TAKES. THAT WILL ALSO MAKE A NICE CLEAN SPOT FOR ALL THE STUFF YOU COLLECT FOR YOUR SALE.)

Your's will be a $5.00 basement, Mrs. Clinger.

O.K., kids, go to it!

2. ASK THE CUSTOMER TO SHOW YOU WHAT THINGS THEY WANT TO KEEP WHEN YOU CLEAN, AND WHAT THINGS THEY WANT TAKEN AWAY. BE SURE TO ASK THEM IF IT IS O.K. TO KEEP SOME OF THE TAKE-AWAYS FOR YOUR SALE. (IF THEY KNOW YOU HAVE A USE FOR IT, THEY MAY DECIDE TO LET YOU TAKE AWAY MORE STUFF.)

3. SORT OUT THE ROOM. PUT THE TAKE-AWAYS INTO BOXES FOR HAULING AWAY, AND THE TRASH INTO TRASH CONTAINERS. STACK THE THINGS TO BE KEPT BY THE CUSTOMER NEATLY IN A CORNER.

4. DUST AND SWEEP THE ROOM.

5. SCRUB ANY SHELVES, DOORS, WINDOWS WITH WATER AND LIQUID SOAP AND BRUSHES OR SPONGES. THEN RINSE WITH CLEAN WATER.

6. MOP THE FLOOR. USE SOAP AND HOT WATER IF POSSIBLE. IF THERE IS GREASE ON THE FLOOR, YOU MAY HAVE TO USE A BRUSH AND SOLVENT, LIKE PAINT THINNER OR "GUNK" FIRST.

7. LAST, ASK YOUR CUSTOMER TO CHECK YOUR WORK BEFORE YOU ASK THEM TO PAY YOU. BE SURE TO HAUL AWAY THE TAKE-AWAYS FOR YOUR SALE RIGHT AWAY. ALSO, BE SURE THE TRASH IS REMOVED FROM THE CLEAN ROOM. THAT'S PART OF THE JOB.

WHEN YOU HAVE COLLECTED LOTS OF BOXES OF TAKE-AWAYS FULL OF GOOD JUNK, THEN IT'S TIME TO THINK ABOUT

IDEA NUMBER **2**: THE GREAT GARAGE SALE

Advertising

Be sure to have your sale on a weekend. Either Saturday, or Saturday and Sunday. Don't choose a holiday weekend. (Too many people go away.) The day before the sale, put little posters up in your neighborhood. (Be sure to take them down when the sale is over.) Use the bulletin boards in laundromats and grocery stores or the library. Put notices up in your school and church. Make a big banner or sign to put up in front on the day of the sale.

Choose a place that is as close as possible to the sidewalk. And be sure it can be seen from the street.

Tell people they can bring things to the sale to trade. (Don't trade something you can sell for another thing you can't.) If it won't bother the neighbors, play music on the radio to make the sale cheery. And if it's convenient, offer coffee or lemonade to people who come. The idea is to make your customers as comfortable and welcome as you can.

THE KIDS' FLEA MARKET

Chances are that when your friends see how successful you are with your garage sale, they'll want to join in the fun. Since garages are limited in space, why not move out to the backyard with your friends and have a Saturday Kids Flea Market. Since you've had experience, you can be the Kids Flea Market manager. Tell your friends to bring their own card tables (or boxes with a board stretched across) to display their sale items. Arrange the tables around the edge of the yard so bargain hunters have lots of room. Encourage a friend to set up a refreshment stand. (Shoppers get hungry.) Be sure your friends ask their parents first before they sell something the parents might not want sold—like old toys, too-small clothes, story books, old jewelry, buttons, tricycles, posters, roller skates, pencils, pens and postcards. Flea Markets really help kids clean their rooms! Speaking of clean—make sure all your friends agree to help you clean up the backyard when the Flea Market closes.

Things To Sell

You need to know that there are two kinds of junk. *Good junk* is what one person asks you to haul away, but another person will pay 10 cents for. But *Junk junk* is what no one wants. Sometimes it's a little hard to know the difference, but it's important to learn if you are going to have a really good garage sale. Here are some examples.

FLOWER POTS: NEW FLOWER POTS ARE EXPENSIVE. SO TAKE ALL THE USED ONES YOU CAN FIND. WASH THEM OUT AND SELL THEM IN SETS AT HALF THE NEW PRICE.

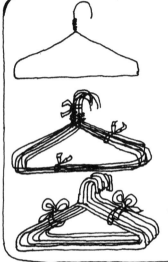

1 WIRE HANGER IS *JUNK JUNK.*

12 WIRE HANGERS NEATLY STACKED AND TIED WITH TWISTEMS IS *GOOD JUNK.* CHARGE 10¢.

12 WOODEN HANGERS NEATLY STACKED AND TIED IS *VERY GOOD JUNK.* CHARGE $1.00.

SMALL FURNITURE ITEMS: SMALL TABLES AND DRESSERS AND WOODEN CHAIRS (THE KITCHEN KIND) ARE GOOD SELLERS. CLEAN THEM UP A LITTLE. PEOPLE LIKE TO REFINISH THEM.

CLOTHES PINS: PUT A DOZEN IN A BAGGIE. TIE THE TOP WITH YARN AND SELL IT FOR 15¢.

LOOSE ITEMS LIKE WOOD SCREWS OR OTHER FASTENERS AREN'T WORTH MUCH. BUT IF YOU COLLECT A JAR OF WOOD SCREWS, YOU CAN SELL IT FOR 25¢. THE SAME IS TRUE FOR BABY FOOD JARS, <u>NATIONAL GEOGRAPHICS</u> AND LOTS OF OTHER THINGS. THEY ARE WORTH MORE IN BUNCHES.

KITCHEN TOOLS: COLLECT WOODEN SPOONS, KNIVES AND OTHER SMALL ITEMS AND SORT THEM BY TYPE. WASH THEM VERY WELL, AND SCOUR THE METAL PARTS TO MAKE THEM BRIGHT.

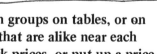

MAGAZINES: ESPECIALLY IF THEY ARE OLD ONES. LOOK FOR OLD <u>GEOGRAPHICS</u>, OLD COPIES OF <u>LIFE</u> AND <u>LOOK</u>, <u>POST</u> OR <u>COLLIERS</u>. SORT THEM BY TITLE AND YEAR. SELL IN SETS.

Arrange your items in groups on tables, or on the floor. Put things that are alike near each other. Be sure to mark prices, or put up a price list. Leave room between things for people to walk around.

Any Timers

ADRIENNE'S I LOVE ANIMALS FACTORY

Adrienne is twelve. But she has been making animal drawings and stuffed animals since she was ten. This year she decided to make big stuffed animal pillows and sell them in a store. Everyone liked them and she sold all she made. Here is what she did.

First she made some big drawings on paper to help her decide about colors and shapes.

Then she cut fabric into the animal shape. She folded the fabric and pinned it to hold it together. She cut the shape through both thicknesses to make a front and a back. She cut the shape big enough to allow for a seam.

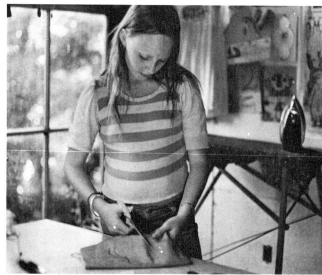

Adrienne sewed up all around the shape except for one side. Then she turned it inside out (to hide the seam).

Then she stuffed the pillow with foam. You can use old rags, or rags and foam mixed. Or use the stuffing from an old pillow or mattress. For small animals, even shredded paper works if you stuff it real tight.

Last, Adrienne sewed up the open side and sewed on eyes, mouth and decorations. Skinny tails or ears can be sewed up without turning inside out, and sewed on the finished animal at the end.

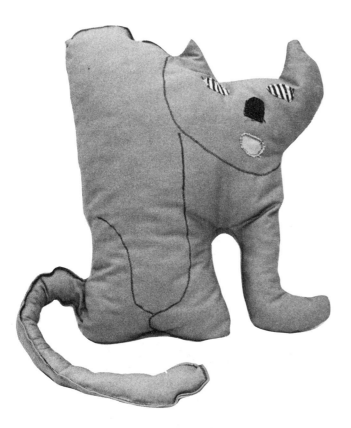

When Adrienne was all done, she made tags for each of her animals. One looked like this.

CRIMSTON
A GreEn MAGiCAL CAT
He's nice to be around when theres no-one else around
Also Arfy a bear and Smack a Mouserab

Any fabric scraps can be used to make animal pillows, but cotton materials like sailcloth or denim are best because they are fairly easy to work with. If you don't have pieces as big as you need, then sew several little ones together and make a patchwork animal pillow.

Adrienne works pretty fast. She designed her first three animal pillows one night and made them all one Saturday. She sold the two little ones for $2.50, and the big one for $4.00.

If you like to sew and can get fabric scraps and a sewing machine from someone, you can have a lot of fun inventing animals and bringing them to life.

You can sell your pillows to your parents' friends. Or you can sell them in stores. If you sell them in a store, the store will add its own share to what they pay you, and sell your pillow for more. This is how stores make their money:

> The store pays you $2.00 for a small pillow.
> It sells the pillow for $3.00 or more.

So if you sell to a store, you may have to sell the pillows for a lower price. But that's okay because a store will usually buy more than one at a time.

The Hot Fudge Sundae and other NEWSPAPERS

This is a picture of Barb Haines. It was taken when she was in the sixth grade and was co-editor of *The Hot Fudge Sundae.* That's a pretty crazy name for a newspaper. Barb and her friend, Nancy Larson, used to get together and write up the news and draw the pictures. (It's a lot more fun to do a paper with friends.) They printed their paper by hand. It was a lot of work. After the pages were done, they tied them with yarn and took the finished papers around to sell. They charged 5 cents each. Here is what *The Hot Fudge Sundae* looked like.

Dear Reader,
White editorials for Big Blob Dean Dill Pickle is open to the public. We would like you to send in stories and poems to Doin Our Own Thing and to...

GO CARTS

Go carts are the new boys on Bruce Street. The present own are Tom Creal, Kevin Terry, and Dickerson. They are made out of wood and are run by lawn mower mo...

THE KNO WHEN POLUT

Graphic Ads

HAPPENING (News)

NEW PUPPIES ON BRUCE ST.

Matt Dickerson's dog Ralph just had puppies. There are seven of them. They wer born Thursday July 10 night, and Friday July 11. One is black, 2are brown and white and 4are black and white. Matt isn't sure what kind of dogs they are, but they aren't pure breeds.

CARNIVAL TO BE ON BRUCE!

There is going to be a carnival at 837 Bruce (Larsons) It will be at about the end of July or the beginning of August. There will be games, food, rides and the coolest fortune telling. There will be signs up, so don't worry

D.B+ B.H.

42

Abigail Brunswutt is in the seventh grade. Her paper is called *The Neighborhood News.* She writes her news on letter-size paper that is folded in half to make pages. Her father takes it to his office where it is printed on a copy machine. Then Abigail folds and staples the pages and takes them to her subscribers. She sells about fifty papers each time for 20 cents each. Her paper comes out once every two weeks. Sort of. Here are some pages.

NEIGHBORHOOD NEWS

20¢

By Abigal Brunswutt

Volume 3.

Can You Beat His Record?

Is what every kid on Lovell avenue has been asking. They are talking about the champion home runner on the M.V. (Mill Valley) seasonal Tiger baseball team. They all want to beat Johnny K. Walker's record of 215 home runs. They all admire him but are all set on beating his record. We asked some of his friends what they thought of him. Some said they weren't interested in beating his record and some were dead set on beating it. Johnny said he will be hitting homers faster than any of the kids can. He also said he wouldn't let any of the other kids catch up with him and he'd keep hitting those homers.

Poor Marcy Sanders

Broke her leg riding her bike. She was riding down her street, (OLD MILL) and a man in a car came streaking down the road and almost hit her. She swirved to the side of the road and hit a parked car and broke her... onlooker... plate na... Marcy ho... Marcy's m... to the e... pital. Marcy was the best Ice Skater on her team. She probably will not be able to skate for at least two more years. Her follies were... up also. T...

She did it!

ALLISON CARTER A young 13 yr. old girl won a 1st place award for the Throckmorton Go-Cart race. She made a huge white Go-Cart. It had a red stripe down its side and the number 49 on each side. She came screeching down the street ahead of all the other carts. Everyone had been rooting for her because she had worked so hard for the championship. She worked on her cart for four weeks straight. She said she would try to win every race they held and build even better carts than she has ever built. She came roaring down the finishing stretch and broke the finish line tape with a grand, finally.

Next race April 7, 1975. 1st and 2nd awards will be given instead of just 1st awards.

THE Wildflower

264

Comics

Mighty Munchkin
By Harry Hu

One day Mighty Munchkin was walking down the river when Charlie Chipmunk said:

Mighty, are you ever going to the park?

It all depends on who else is going with us.

Well, Betty Bird can come and so can Sally Snake.

OK Now lets go!

hello

this is real fun!

yah a real gas.

awk, awk, S, S, S, S

are you o.k. Charlie are you o.k.?

awk awk S, S, S, S, S

So Charlie couldn't walk and couldn't even get up. So, Mighty Munchkin went behind a tree and came out with two M's on the front.

He picked up Charlie and flew off up into the sky towards the sun. Find out next week where Mighty is taking Charlie Remember Next week!

SEXY SEXY SALLY
By Andrea H.

It started in a saloon in Texas. Sally came riding into town on a big white gelding. Everyone stared with wonder.

SALOON SALOON

Hi ya Sally

Hi ya Sally how's everything?

Howdy fellas whats up?

You Can Start Your Own Paper

Here is what you need. First, you need to like to write stories and make pictures. If you do, and if you have a nose for news, you've got almost everything you need.

Next you need a name. *You can call your paper anything you like. But it should be a name that people can remember, and won't be confused with grownup papers. It might help to use a name that tells people it's about their neighborhood. Like* The Pearl Street Gazette. *Or* The Sun Valley Neighbor. *Or* The East Diversey Street Bugle.

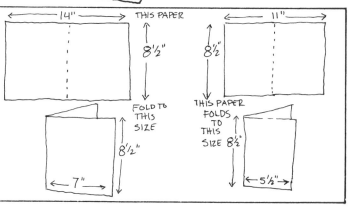

Next you should decide how big to make your paper. And here is some good advice: Start Small. No one will mind. If you try to make your paper too big, you just might not ever finish it at all. Choose a size that is standard size for paper. Here are two standard sizes: Both these sizes go with: carbon paper, copy machines, mimeograph machines and printing presses.

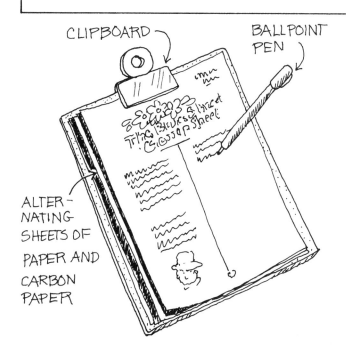

CLIPBOARD

BALLPOINT PEN

ALTER-NATING SHEETS OF PAPER AND CARBON PAPER

Now you should probably decide how you will print your paper. *If you don't know anyone with a copy machine, or a mimeograph, or a printing press, then you should start by printing your paper with carbon paper. (It might be a good idea anyway until you've done a few issues and have more experience.) Carbon paper is just a way to make more than one copy when you write the news. You can make five or six copies each time, then start over and write again.*

You'll get tired of carbon paper pretty soon. But by that time you'll know that you like doing a newspaper and your neighbors will know they like reading it. Then it makes sense to expand your business by printing more pages and more copies. You can do that by taking your paper all written to someplace where there is a copy machine. Or you can write your news on mimeograph stencils and have them run off in the church or school office, or wherever you can find a mimeo machine.

Now you need NEWS. And here is where your imagination is important. Since all the grownup papers are filled with mostly bad news, maybe your paper should concentrate on telling people mostly good news. (In fact, *Mostly Good News* isn't a bad idea for a name.) Here are some kinds of good news people around your neighborhood might like very much to know about:

There will be a bake sale next Saturday at the Baptist Church. Mrs Strout says she will make one of her famous pecan pies which will be auctioned off to the highest bidder. Last year, a man from Temple Street bought the...

Mrs Holmes' dog Susu has had puppies. They came last Sunday morning just as Mr. Holmes was backing the car out to go to church. Mother and babies are doing well. The father is unknown but he must have had black spots. Mrs Holmes hopes her friends will come and see the dogs because they are very... she wants to give... call 772-476...

Ester Hendley has returned from her vacation. She is the only person in the neighborhood who has ever... Africa. Her father... slides of their... day evening at 7:30... in the neighbor... invited to come... them.

Mr Appleyard tells us that last week a night-time visitor to his backyard knocked over the garbage can. This is the third time it has happened. Anyone else having the same problem please tell this newspaper... can get to the bottom of it. (UGH.)

How To Get Good News

Every neighborhood is different. You'll have to invent your own methods for getting news. But here are some hints. In every town there are certain people who know lots about what is going on. Get to know who they are and tell them you want their help. Make up some little cards with your phone number that people can tack by their phones. When they think of good news, they can call you.

Be sure to call every club or other organization in your neighborhood. Tell the president of each one that you will print their club events and news in your paper. Call them regularly to check. Also check with your police or dog pound for news of lost items or dogs (or found ones). Check the school office each week for news. Also the library for special events. And all the churches. Soon you'll have more good news than you have space to print.

About Money

A newspaper won't make much money at first. But if you keep it going and people get used to seeing it, and find out about it from their friends, you will be able to print more copies and then you will make more money. Don't take money in advance from your readers. It's better to sell each issue as you deliver it.

After you have been in business a while, you can think about trying to sell small ads to local merchants. Advertising space in newspapers is sold by the inch, or by the piece of a page. Make up a price sheet that shows your rates, and keep your prices low. A dollar for a half or a third of a page is probably as much as you should ever charge.

You may not know this, but lots of grownups are cuckoo about kids' artwork. I don't know why. Maybe it's because most kids aren't afraid to draw and grownups wish they were like that, too. Here is a way you can make some money and have a lot of fun by making art shows for grownups. You and your friends can start a Kids Art Company. Your Company can make shows to go wherever there are empty, boring walls to look at.

Think about all the places people have to be all day with nothing nice to look at. Places like doctors' offices. Or banks. Or the post office or the public library. Take some of your best drawings or paintings to the people in charge of these places. Tell each one that you can bring a bright and colorful show of ten pieces of kids' art for a month for only $5. Also tell the person in charge that he or she can sell each painting for $1 and keep half the money. (That way, the show doesn't cost anything for the month, and you could earn extra money.) Here's how that works: When you put up the show, charge $5. After one month, come back. Take away the art that wasn't sold. Collect half the money for the art that was sold. If the whole show was sold ($1 x 10 paintings = $10), your customer keeps $5 and you collect another $5.

Be sure the drawings and paintings are your very best ones. People can tell if you whip up a batch of things just to make a show. Choose carefully. Make sure there is a mixture of sizes and colors. And most important, be sure you figure out a way to prepare your drawings or paintings for the show. Each one should be glued or fastened to something that can be hung on a wall and look nice. (See the suggestions below.) Be sure each piece has the artist's name on it.

Getting Your Show Ready

Below are two ways for you to get your drawings and paintings ready to hang in the art show. This is a very important part of your business. It should be done carefully.

This is important: Near the show when it is hanging, there should be a little sign that explains where it came from. You might make one that says something like this ————————→

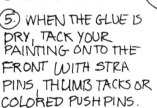

These PAINTINGs were put here by kids to cheer you up. They are for sale for $1.00 each. Please ask if you want to buy one.

---

① TAKE A PIECE OF CORRUGATED CARDBOARD, AT LEAST AN INCH SMALLER THAN YOUR PAINTING ON ALL SIDES. PLACE IT ON THE BACK OF YOUR ART. CUT THE FOUR CORNERS ←HERE→

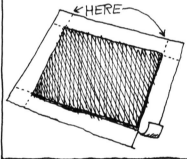

② FOLD THE PAINTING OVER THE CARDBOARD AND GLUE IT DOWN WITH WHITE GLUE.

③ WRAP THE WHOLE THING SMOOTHLY WITH PLASTIC WRAP.

④ NOW COVER THE BACK WITH A PIECE OF PAPER THE SAME SIZE AS THE CARDBOARD. GLUE IT DOWN.

⑤ GLUE A PICTURE HOOK ON THE BACK. BE SURE IT IS IN THE CENTER, NEAR THE TOP.

---

① CUT OUT A SIDE OF A CARDBOARD BOX, ONE THAT IS IN PRETTY GOOD SHAPE.

② THIN SOME WHITE GLUE WITH ENOUGH WATER SO THAT IT PAINTS ONTO THE CARDBOARD EASILY AND COVER ONE SIDE WITH IT.

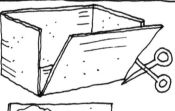

③ CAREFULLY PLACE THE BOARD GLUE-SIDE-DOWN ON A PIECE ON CLOTH LARGER THAN IT IS AND FAIRLY THIN.

④ PAINT GLUE ON THE OVERLAPPING PART OF THE CLOTH AND FOLD IT NEATLY OVER THE BACK OF THE BOARD.

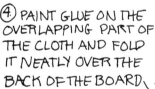

⑤ WHEN THE GLUE IS DRY, TACK YOUR PAINTING ON TO THE FRONT WITH STRAIGHT PINS, THUMB TACKS OR COLORED PUSH PINS.

⑥ TO HANG IT, ATTACH STICK-ON PICTURE HOOKS TO THE BACK AND ADD STRING.

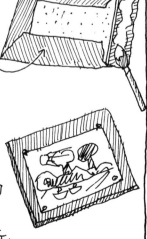

KEILA'S OWLS

Keila Diehl is ten years old and likes to do macrame. Her parents own a little gift shop. So Keila has put the two together and is making little macrame necklaces that look like owls and selling them in her parents' store. She says that now that she's got the hang of it, it only takes her about fifteen minutes to make an owl. If you know how to macrame and you think you'd like to give Keila's owls a try, here are some step-by-step pictures to show you how. All of the knots are half hitches, except for the nose, which is made of square knots.

You'll need a board to work on, and some straight pins. This helps to keep your work neat and it's easier for you to see what you're doing. You'll also need a ball of twine, macrame cord or heavy string, two beads for eyes, and a small stick for the owl's feet to be tied to. You'll get a lot of different personalities for your owls by using different kinds of cord and beads.

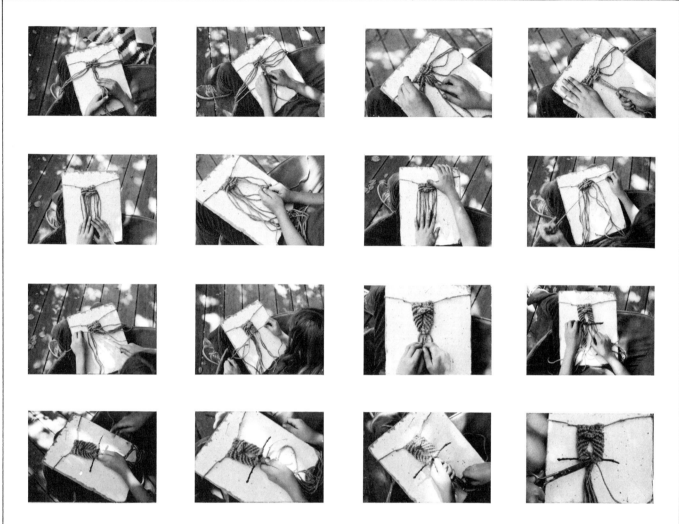

Selling Your Owls

You could sell your owls at church bazaars or local flea markets or take them to stores and sell them on consignment. That's what Keila does at her parents' store. It means that the store only pays you when they sell something of yours, and if they don't sell something after a certain period of time, you have to take it back. Usually they keep from one-third to one-half of the money paid for an item. Keila's owls

sell for $2.50. She gets $1.50 of that and her parents, the store owners, keep $1.00.

Make a nice display for your owls to take around to shops you think might be interested. Make eight or ten owls, all different if possible, and pin them to a board. Use a piece of corrugated cardboard or Celotex and cover it with a pretty piece of dark material. Make a little sign that says who made them.

The Afterschool Glassworks

Crash! Next time someone in your house breaks a drinking glass, think about this idea. People are breaking drinking glasses everywhere. Probably every minute someone breaks one. But that's not all. Everywhere, people throw away perfectly good glass jars and bottles that could be made into useful things. Like drinking glasses. You can do it. It's easy. You can get the bottles for nothing. And you can sell the things you make. What more could you ask? Someone breaks a drinking glass. You come along and say:

HEY MISTER! WE CAN TURN YOUR OLD BEER BOTTLES OR WINE JUGS INTO USEFUL AND HANDSOME THINGS LIKE A DRINKING GLASS TO REPLACE THE ONE YOU JUST BROKE. WANT TO SEE OUR SAMPLES?

WE COLLECT OLD BOTTLES AND JUGS

GLASSES FOR SALE

Right away, you have made good sense. You have offered to take away the bottles that are cluttering up the kitchen. And what's more, you have offered to turn them into something useful. All of a sudden, you're irresistable. And if your customer doesn't want to buy, you can take his or her bottles, make them into drinking glasses (or other things) and sell them to the people next door. How can you miss?

WHOOPS!

Here are some of the things you can make:

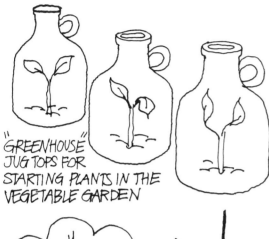

"GREENHOUSE" JUG TOPS FOR STARTING PLANTS IN THE VEGETABLE GARDEN

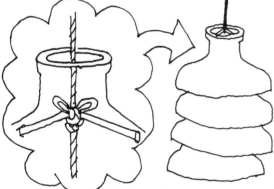

BOTTLE TOP WINDCHIMES
TIE A PIECE OF BENT WIRE INSIDE EACH ONE TO MAKE A HANGER

A FISH BOWL FROM A JUG BOTTOM

OR A SALAD BOWL

DON'T FORGET TO SAND ALL CUT EDGES SMOOTH!

A SET OF JUICE GLASSES, SMALL, OR MILK GLASSES, BIGGER

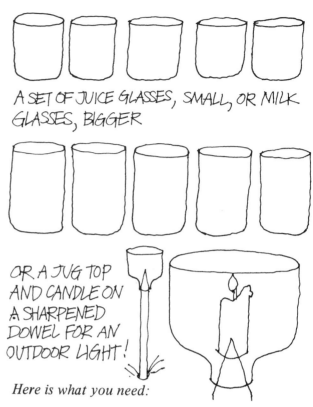

OR A JUG TOP AND CANDLE ON A SHARPENED DOWEL FOR AN OUTDOOR LIGHT!

Here is what you need:

Something to cut the bottles and jugs with. The easiest tool to use is a special bottle cutter. The one we have is called a Fleming Cutter and it costs about $8. It is made by the Fleming Bottle and Jug Cutter Inc., Seattle, Washington 98188. Craft stores and some hardware stores carry cutters like these. $8 is a lot of money, but it's worth saving up for if you can use it to make hundreds of things you can sell.

You'll need a good place to work near some light. It should be a place that is away from small children who might cut themselves on the cut edges of the glass (before you sand them smooth). And it should be a place that can be easily swept clean of any glass pieces. (Sometimes even the best bottle cutters break one.)

And don't forget. You'll never run out of customers. Because as long as there are drinking glasses, people will break them. (Crash!)

NICK HALE'S BIKE SHOP

If you like bikes and know about how they work, you should think hard about starting your own garage or backyard bike shop. That's what Nick Hale did. He made money and had a good time working on broken bikes, buying junked bikes and making them like new. You can do the same thing. Here are some of Nick Hale's ideas about how to get started.

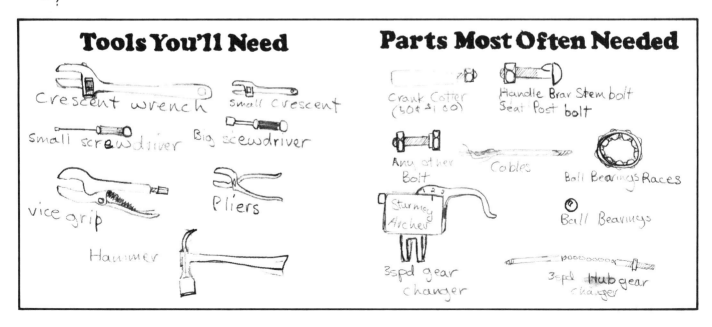

Tools You'll Need

Crescent wrench

small crescent

small screwdriver

Big screwdriver

vice grip

Pliers

Hammer

Parts Most Often Needed

Crank Cotter (50¢ $1.00)

Handle Brar Stem bolt
Seat Post bolt

Any other Bolt

Cables

Ball Bearings Races

Sturmey Archer

Ball Bearings

3spd gear changer

3-spd Hub gear changer

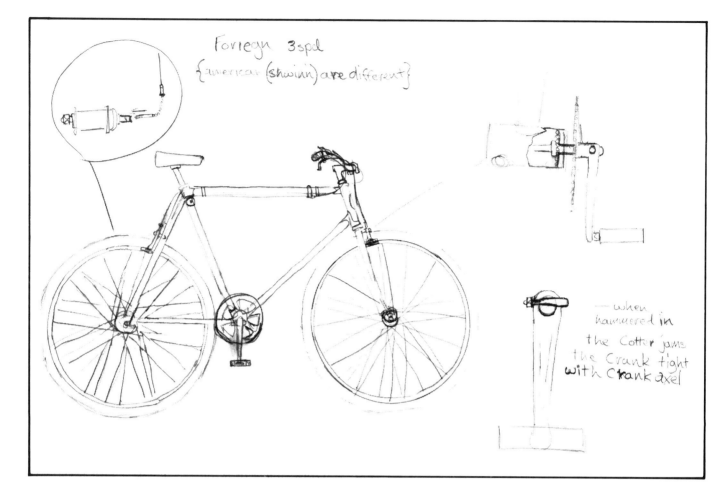

Foriegn 3spd
{american (shwinn) are different}

when hammered in
the Cotter jams
the Crank tight
with Crank axel

Here are some things to think about if you are going to collect parts and rebuild bikes or repair them.

1. Start with your own bike. Take it apart and put it back together again. If you're not sure, watch someone at another bike shop do it first. Don't be afraid to ask questions.

2. Stick with 3 speeds. Ten speed bikes are too complicated and not worth the time. Also, you're more apt to find old 3 speeds around.

3. If someone asks you to convert a 3 speed to a 10 speed, don't do it, It's very difficult and not worth the time and trouble.

4. Get parts from junk yards. That is the cheapest place, unless you get them free from people who are throwing them away.

5. Try to stick to one or two popular makes (like Schwinn or Raleigh). It will take longer to assemble parts that way, but you'll save in the long run because you're sure to be able to use everything you find.

6. Make the rounds asking for old junk bikes. Lots of people have them, never use them and would just as soon sell or give them away. An old 3 speed with most of its parts can usually be had for $5. If you strip it down, clean it, replace broken parts and repaint it, you can easily get $15 or $20 for it.

7. The painting is very important. Maybe the most important part. People are much more apt to buy a bike that is nicely painted than one that works just as well, but hasn't been repainted, so be sure to take the time to do that part very carefully.

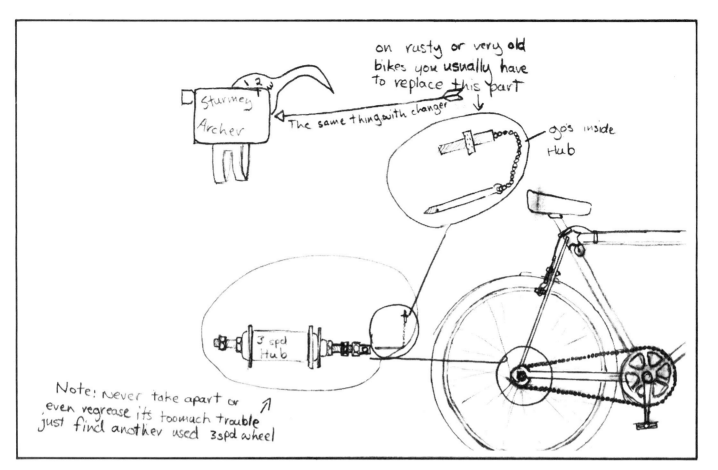

on rusty or very old bikes you usually have to replace this part

The same thing with changer

Sturmey Archer

go's inside Hub

3 spd Hub

Note: Never take apart or even regrease its too much trouble, just find another used 3spd wheel

8.   There are several pretty good bike repair books out. Get one that deals with the kind of bike you are going to work with and keep it handy as a reference. You'll need it, especially at first.

9.   You'll also need some money to start with. You'll need it for tools, and for buying old bikes and bike parts. Nick started with $50 that he saved from a paper route.

10.   Find a good place to work. It should have places for storing bikes and bike parts, and it should be dry. If there is moisture, bike parts will rust.

Should be 21 Ball-Bearings

HEADSET

KAP!
KAP!

When Painting Frame remove ball bearing cups because you would probably want to keep the crome

to remove Tap lightly all the way round until drops off

JON'S CORSAGES

Once upon a time there was a kid named Jon who figured out a great way to make people happy on special celebration days, and make some money for himself doing it. He would phone the husbands in his neighborhood when their wives weren't home. He'd say something like this:

Hello, Mr. Finster, this is Jon Wilson. I'm selling corsages for birthdays or anniversaries. If you order one now for your wife, I'll get it from the Chelsea Flower Shop and deliver it to you on the day of the special occasion. It'll cost $2.00.

You could pick it up at my house if you want to make sure it's a surprise.

Then the husband might say:

Great! I can surprise my wife and not have to bother getting a corsage from the florist myself!

Oh Chester! For Me??

Jon talked to different flower shops ahead of time to find one that would agree to his project. The one he found wanted $1.50 for each corsage, so Jon charged $2.00 and made 50 cents with each order. He also found out how far in advance the flower shop needed his order.

This worked so well he did the same thing at Christmastime with wreaths. This was a little easier because it wasn't a surprise and he could take orders door-to-door.

If you think this would be a good project for you, you might consider doing it at Valentine's Day, Mother's Day or Easter. Or you could order bouquets instead of corsages. Just be sure to plan enough ahead of the holiday.

The Sometimes Sew and Patchworks

This is an idea that is good any time. It's something to do when there's nothing to do. When it's raining outside. When you are getting over the flu and feel fine but can't go out for two days. Or when you're just plain bored. All you need is an old-time all-around jumble-dump rag-bag.

You know. That big bag of scraps that your mom has in the closet that she never uses but won't throw away. You know the one.

Well, tell her it's really a natural resource in disguise and that you're going to make a miracle out of it. (No one can resist a miracle.) Then get a needle and thread and try making one of these sure-fire scrap recipes.

PURSE

① PATCH TOGETHER ENOUGH STRIPS OR ODD-SIZED PIECES OF COLORFUL CLOTH TO MAKE A RECTANGULAR PIECE 6" X 14."

② LINE YOUR PATCHED PIECE WITH A SOLID COLORED RECTANGLE OF MATERIAL THE SAME SIZE.

③ FOLD LIKE THIS →

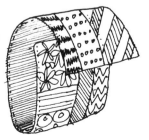

④ ATTACH A RIBBON 2" X 48" TO THE SIDES OF YOUR PURSE LIKE THIS:

⑤ SEW ON A LARGE SNAP OR MAKE A LOOP AND SEW ON A BUTTON IF YOU WANT YOUR PURSE TO CLOSE.

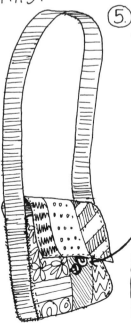

☆ If you don't want to use a ribbon, make a strap by piecing together a 48" X 4" strip of patches. Fold it lengthwise and sew together. Turn it inside out, sew to the purse.

SKIRT

1. MEASURE YOUR WAIST, AND MEASURE FROM YOUR WAIST TO WHERE YOU WANT YOUR SKIRT TO END. ADD 3" TO THE LENGTH MEASUREMENT (FOR THE ELASTIC CASING AND THE HEM.)

A GATHERED SKIRT IS USUALLY 2 TIMES YOUR WAIST MEASUREMENT, SO MULTIPLY YOUR WAIST SIZE BY 2.

> EXAMPLE OF MATH:
> WAIST = 20"
> 2 × 20" = 40"
> LENGTH OF SKIRT = 36"
> 36" + 3" = 39"

NOTE: IF YOU DON'T WANT A REALLY FULL SKIRT THEN MULTIPLY YOUR WAIST MEASUREMENT BY 1½". EXAMPLE: 1½ × 20" = 30".

2. PATCH TOGETHER ENOUGH BRIGHT COLORED SQUARES TO MAKE A RECTANGULAR PIECE THAT'S THE SAME AS YOUR MATH.

3. SEW THIS SEAM

4. FOLD THE TOP EDGE DOWN ½", IRON FLAT, THEN FOLD DOWN AGAIN 1", IRON, PIN OR BASTE AND SEW.

BE SURE TO LEAVE A 2" OPENING SO YOU CAN THREAD THROUGH A PIECE OF 3/4" ELASTIC THAT'S EXACTLY THE MEASUREMENT OF YOUR WAIST.

WHEN YOU'VE FINISHED PULLING THE ELASTIC THROUGH THE CASING, OVERLAP THE TWO ENDS OF THE ELASTIC ABOUT 1". SEW THEM TIGHTLY TOGETHER, TUCK THE ELASTIC BACK INSIDE THE CASING, SEW UP THE OPENING IN THE CASING.

5. NOW THE HEM. FOLD BOTTOM EDGE ½" UNDER, IRON AND FOLD UNDER AGAIN 1", IRON AND SEW.

APRON

1. PATCH TOGETHER A SERIES OF BRIGHT COLORED SQUARES OF FABRIC TO MAKE A SQUARE PIECE THAT MEASURES 20"X20".

2. FOLD THE TOP EDGE UNDER ½", IRON FLAT, THEN FOLD AGAIN 1", IRON AND SEW.

3. PULL A 36" RIBBON THROUGH THE CASING.

4. HEM THE BOTTOM EDGE BY TURNING UNDER ½", IRON FLAT, TURN UNDER ANOTHER 1", IRON AND SEW.

HOT PAD

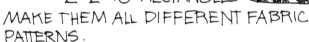

1. CUT: 4 - 2" SQUARES
   2 - 2"X 4" RECTANGLES
   2 - 2"X 8" RECTANGLES

MAKE THEM ALL DIFFERENT FABRIC PATTERNS.

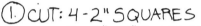

2. SEW ALL THE 2" SQUARES TOGETHER TO MAKE A SQUARE.
SEW ONE OF THE 2"X4" RECTANGLES ON THE TOP OF THE SQUARE AND THE OTHER ON THE BOTTOM.
SEW THE 2"X 8" RECTANGLES TO EACH SIDE OF THE SQUARE. IRON FLAT.

3. CUT A SQUARE OF MATERIAL THAT MATCHES THE TOP PATCHED SQUARE.

4. TURN RIGHT SIDES IN, SEW 3 SIDES OF THE HOT PAD. TURN RIGHT SIDES OUT. IRON FLAT.

5. FILL WITH COTTON BATTING OR POLYESTER.

6. SEW UP THE LAST SIDE.
SEW ON A PLASTIC RING OR A CLOTH LOOP

PLACE MAT

1. PATCH TOGETHER 12-4" SQUARES LIKE THIS.

2. CUT A BACK PIECE OR LINING TO FIT THE TOP PIECE.

3. TURN RIGHT SIDES IN. SEW 3 SIDES. TURN OUT, IRON FLAT.

4. PRESS DOWN FINAL SIDE 5/8" TO HIDE THE RAW EDGE. TUCK INSIDE AND SEW.

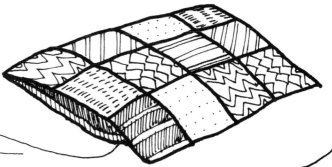

LUNCH BAG

1. PATCH TOGETHER ENOUGH SQUARES AND STRIPS OF FABRIC TO MAKE A RECTANGLE 10"x22".

(FOLD)

2. TURN THE TOP AND BOTTOM EDGES UNDER 1/2", IRON, TURN UNDER 1", IRON AND SEW TO FORM A CASING ON EACH END.

3. FOLD IN THE CENTER WITH RIGHT SIDE IN. SEW UP SIDE SEAMS TO 1" OF TOP.

4. TURN OUT. THREAD A STRING THROUGH EACH CASING. TIE ENDS OF STRINGS INTO KNOTS.

5. GATHER STRINGS TO CLOSE BAG.

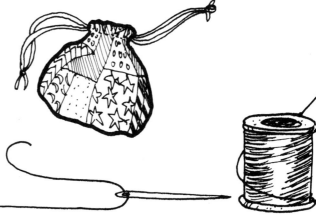

Once you've tried a couple or so of these and you like what happens, get some friends to help make more. Try it on a Saturday morning or a vacation day. Get everyone around a big table and divide up the work. If everyone has a good time, and wants to do it again, you've got yourself a Patchworks. Keep track of how much each person does so you can pay each one when you sell your work. You could keep a Patchworks Book with a page for each person. That way your worker-friends can work any time they have a chance. Each one enters a record of what they make on their own page. A page might look like this:

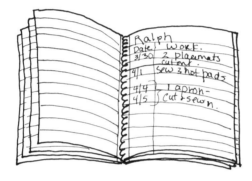

When you have made a few of each item, take them around to some stores. Good places to try are gift shops, toy stores, book shops, etc. Make a little box (see the instructions on the next page) for your things to sit on a counter in. Be sure there is a sign on the box telling everyone who made the Patchworks.

Ask the store owner how much he or she thinks you should charge for each item. If you think the price sounds right, and if the store owner is willing, let them take your Patchworks on consignment. That means they sell the things and pay you after. And they keep some of the money in exchange for selling your stuff.

HERE ARE SOME WAYS TO SELL YOUR PATCHWORKS:
AT ANY LOCAL P.T.A. CAKE SALE OR OTHER GATHERING.
AT FLEA MARKETS.
ADVERTISE IN NEIGHBORHOOD SHOPPING NEWSPAPERS.
MAKE COLORFUL SIGNS FOR LAUNDROMATS AND MARKET BULLETIN BOARDS.

HOW TO MAKE AN ALL-PURPOSE BOX

THIS IS A GOOD BOX TO MAKE IF YOU WANT SOMETHING THAT LOOKS CLEANER AND NEATER THAN AN OLD CARDBOARD BOX YOU MIGHT FIND AROUND THE HOUSE. ALSO, YOU CAN MAKE IT ANY SIZE YOU WANT. TO DO A REALLY NICE JOB, YOU'LL NEED TO USE A MATTE KNIFE, A STRAIGHT-EDGE AND VERY HEAVY PAPER OR CARDBOARD.

A MATTE KNIFE HAS A VERY SHARP BLADE. GET A GROWNUP TO SHOW YOU HOW TO USE ONE.

THE BEST STRAIGHT EDGE IS A METAL RULER, BUT IF YOU'RE CAREFUL, ANY RULER WILL DO. YOU USE THIS AGAINST THE EDGE OF THE KNIFE TO KEEP IT CUTTING IN A STRAIGHT LINE.

BUY A SHEET OF CARDBOARD OR HEAVY PAPER FROM AN ART SUPPLY STORE. TELL THE CLERK WHAT YOU WANT TO USE IT FOR AND THEY CAN HELP YOU CHOOSE.

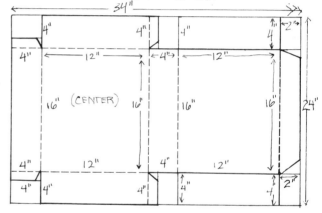

LET'S SAY YOU WANT TO MAKE A BOX 16" x 12", AND 4" DEEP. DRAW LINES ON YOUR CARDBOARD LIKE THE PICTURE ABOVE. CUT ON THE SOLID LINES AND FOLD TOWARD THE CENTER ON THE DOTTED LINES. NOW GLUE OR TAPE THE LITTLE FLAPS TO THE BOX SIDES. (IF YOU WANT PRACTICE FIRST, MAKE A SMALL BOX OUT OF PAPER)

START YOUR OWN
Neighborhood Nursery

Here is how to grow and sell indoor plants. If you like to make things grow, it could be a fine after school business. . . . .

Will It Work?

Most people don't take the trouble to start their own plants. If yours are healthy, not too expensive, and especially if the containers look good, you will have no trouble selling them. You can include instructions for watering and other care. Charge 50¢ for small plants, and up to $1.00 for larger ones, or ones with blooms, or plants that come with hangers.

How Much Can You Make?

Income from selling 40 plants at 50¢ each . . . $20.00

Cost of soil	$2.00
Cost of Rootone	1.00
What You Spend	$3.00
What You Make	$17.00

What You Need:

1. **Cuttings** which you get from plants that are already growing.

2. **Dirt.** If you live in a city, you may have to buy potting soil. A bag containing 1 cubic foot—enough for 40 plants—costs about $2.00.

3. **Containers.** Any small container, like cut-off milk cartons or small tin cans. Don't buy them. Find them.

4. **A growing place.** Could be any sheltered place that has good light and isn't too cold: a sunny window sill; an enclosed porch; a fire escape or balcony; or a table by a window.

5. **Root hormone.** You may need it. Roots will grow from cuttings without it, but it helps plants get a good start. You can buy a package of Rootone for about $1.00, and that's enough for 100 plants.

6. **Time.** It will take about two weeks for cuttings to root and get big and strong enough to sell.

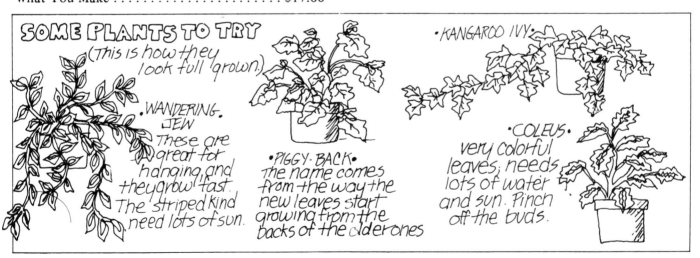

SOME PLANTS TO TRY
(This is how they look full grown.)

·WANDERING JEW·
These are great for hanging, and they grow fast. The striped kind need lots of sun.

·PIGGY-BACK·
The name comes from the way the new leaves start growing from the backs of the older ones

·KANGAROO IVY·

·COLEUS·
very colorful leaves; needs lots of water and sun. Pinch off the buds.

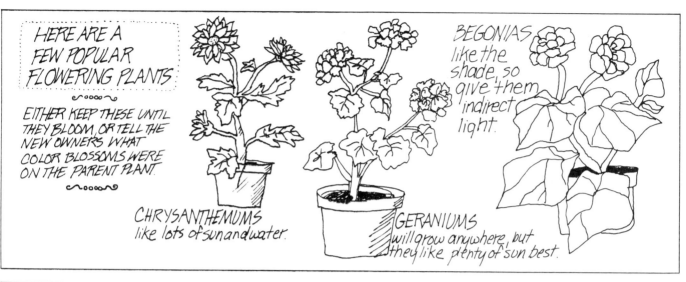

HERE ARE A FEW POPULAR FLOWERING PLANTS

EITHER KEEP THESE UNTIL THEY BLOOM, OR TELL THE NEW OWNERS WHAT COLOR BLOSSOMS WERE ON THE PARENT PLANT.

CHRYSANTHEMUMS like lots of sun and water.

GERANIUMS will grow anywhere, but they like plenty of sun best.

BEGONIAS like the shade, so give them indirect light.

How To Do It

Start by taking a cutting from a big and healthy house plant—your home's, a neighbor's, or from a friendly nursery if they will let you. Use scissors to cut off a piece 2 or 3 inches long. Pull off the bottom leaves and put the stem in a jar of lukewarm water, like this. Half the stem should be in the water. You can dip the end in a little Rootone if you want to.

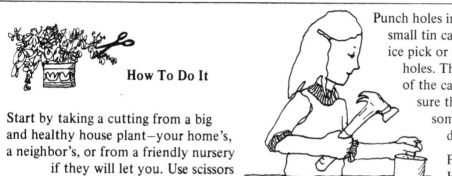

You can put several cuttings in one wide jar, but be sure the roots have room to grow. You'll see them beginning in 2 or 3 days at the bottom of the stem. Check every day to make sure there is enough water in the jar. In about 2 weeks, or when the roots are about 3 inches long, plant your cuttings in containers.

Be sure you have good rich soil. If you can't find any nearby, buy some potting soil.

Punch holes in the bottom of your containers—small tin cans, or cut-off milk cartons—with an ice pick or hammer and nails. Make about 10 holes. These holes allow water to drain out of the can when you water your plants, so be sure they are sitting on a bowl, plate or something like that so the water won't drip on the table or floor.

Fill the cans about half full of dirt. Hold your cutting in the can and put in more dirt, almost to the top. Tap the soil gently down so the plant can stand up on its own. Water the plants and put them in a sunny or very bright window. Wait a few days to be sure they are healthy. Then they're ready to sell.

Some people grow cuttings right in the dirt (and don't use a jar of water) by covering the tip of the cutting with Rootone and planting directly in the dirt. If you do this, water well to activate the Rootone.

If you like to grow plants from seeds, you can use an old egg carton. Fill the holes with dirt, plant the seeds, and keep damp.

DECORATING YOUR CANS & CARTONS

MAKE THEM PRETTY WHILE YOU WAIT FOR THE CUTTINGS TO ROOT.....

YOU CAN WRAP STICKY-BACKED SHELF PAPER AROUND THEM IF THERE'S ANY EXTRA AROUND YOUR HOUSE, OR BUY A ROLL AT THE DIME-STORE IF YOU'RE GOING TO DO A LOT OF THEM.

— OR —

PAINT THE CANS WITH ANY LEFT-OVER OIL-BASE PAINT YOU OR YOUR NEIGHBORS MIGHT HAVE AROUND.

NAME YOUR PLANTS

AND MAKE NICE LITTLE INTRODUCTION CARDS FOR THEM. INCLUDE THE COMMON AND BIOLOGICAL NAMES AND A FEW TIPS ON CARE.

THIS IS DENISE. SHE IS A NEW COLEUS. (COLEUS BLUMEI). SHE NEEDS STRONG, DIRECT SUN & LOTS OF WATER. BE SURE TO PINCH OFF HER BUDS.

MAKE A HANGER

TIE 3 TWO-FOOT LONG STRANDS OF HEAVY STRING TOGETHER AT BOTH ENDS; USE GOOD KNOTS. THEN ADD A 4TH STRING TIED TO THE OTHERS TO FIT AROUND THE MIDDLE OF THE CAN, SO THE STRINGS ARE SPACED EVENLY APART. DECORATE BY STRING-ING ON BEADS, BEANS, MACARONI, BUTTONS, OR WHATEVER YOU THINK OF.

SOME OTHER PROJECTS TO TRY

PEOPLE MIGHT LIKE TO BUY THESE FOR GIFTS.

A CACTUS GARDEN

CACTUS AND SUCCULENT PLANTS START WELL FROM CUTTINGS. LET THEM DRY FOR 2 WEEKS AND THEN JUST STICK THEM IN A MIXTURE OF ½ SAND AND ½ DIRT. USE ANY SHALLOW CONTAINER, LIKE PIE TINS OR FROZEN FOOD TRAYS. ADD LITTLE SHELLS AND STONES.

HERBS

THESE ARE EASY TO START FROM SEEDS, WHICH ARE CHEAP TO BUY. READ THE PACKAGES TO FIND OUT HOW LONG THEY'LL TAKE TO START. PLANT 6 OR 7 SEEDS IN A CAN OF DIRT AND LABEL EACH CAN. MINT, PARSLEY AND CHIVES ARE ALL EASY TO GROW AND VERY POPULAR. SELL THEM AS A SET IN A FROZEN-FOOD TIN.

START AVOCADO TREES

GENTLY WASH AND DRY THE SEED FROM A RIPE AVOCADO. BALANCE IT IN A JAR OF WARMISH WATER BY STICKING 3 OR 4 TOOTHPICKS IN THE SIDE. PUT THE SEED IN WATER, FAT SIDE DOWN, AND KEEP IT IN A DARK, DRAFT-FREE PLACE, LIKE A CUPBOARD. PLANT WHEN THE NEW STEM IS A FEW INCHES TALL. LEAVE THE TOP OF THE SEED SHOWING.

HOW TO SELL YOUR PLANTS

Door to Door. *Make a little tray for your plants from a box lid and visit the neighbors. This will give you an idea of how people like your plants. Listen to what they say. When someone doesn't buy one, try to figure out why. That will help you do better next time.*

At A Flea Market or Garage Sale. *The next time there is a bazaar or garage sale in your neighborhood, take along a little table, a sign and some of your plants. This is a good time to sell the ones with fancy containers or hangers you've been working on.*

At A Neighborhood Shop. *If your corner grocery has space on a counter, put out a few plants and a sign. Be sure your sign tells people this is a kid business. Ask the store man to sell your plants for you and let him keep one third of what he sells.*

IF YOUR NURSERY IS A SUCCESS... TRY MAKING BOTTLE GARDENS.... A PLANTS BOOK FROM THE LIBRARY CAN SHOW YOU HOW.

THE HAND and FOOT PRINTER

HANDMADE GIFT CARDS, WRAPPING PAPER, STATIONERY ETC PRINTED HERE. REASONABLE RATES 15 CEDAR STREET.

You already know what a printer does. But did you know that there are lots of kids who have printing presses in their basements (or attics or garages) and make all their own spending money by printing things for people? And did you know that if you want to have a print shop you could start one without having to buy any printing press or type or other tools that cost a lot of money? Well, you can, and here's how.

The Potato Press

What you will need: One large potato (the kind with brown skin). A small tube of water-base block printing ink. A small knife.

First make a design with pencil on paper. Be sure your design is simple because you are going to cut it into the potato. Solid shapes work best. Then copy the design onto the potato by scratching the shapes lightly onto a freshly cut

place. Now carefully cut away all the potato that is *not* part of your design. Cut down about 1/8 or 1/4 inch. Now you have made a potato stamp. The rest of the potato is your "handle."

Squeeze a dab of ink the size of a big pea onto a piece of paper and smear it out a little. (Or use a small rubber ink roller if you have one.) Press the potato gently into the ink two or three times to make sure the design is covered.

Now press the potato firmly *straight down* onto a piece of smooth paper. And there you have it.

Things You Can Make With a Potato Press

A potato press is just right for making small sheets of wrapping paper for small packages. Buy a roll of plain white shelf paper at the supermarket. (Be sure to get the paper kind, not the plastic.) You can cut this paper into sheets and print them with potato stamps in many patterns and colors. Sell ten sheets for 50 cents. Be sure to include with each ten sheets, ten tiny gift cards made from the same potato stamps.

WRAPPING PAPER WITH POTATO SHAPE PRINTED MANY TIMES

GIFT CARD TO GO WITH IT

You can make stationery for your friends. Cut their initials or their favorite design into the potato. If you cut letter shapes, be sure to cut them *backwards* into the potato, so they will read *frontwards* when you print them. Print ten plain dime store sheets and ten envelopes for 50 cents or more, depending on the cost of paper.

The Linoleum Press

If you have tried potato printing and want to print larger things, then you should try printing from linoleum blocks. These are more expensive and harder to cut, but they're worth the extra cost and effort. What you will need: Some linoleum blocks (buy them already on wood blocks at the art store, or make them yourself). A set of cutting tools. A small tube of ink. And a little rubber ink roller.

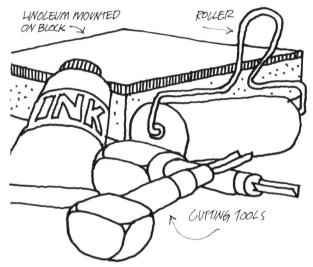

LINOLEUM MOUNTED ON BLOCK

ROLLER

INK

CUTTING TOOLS

If there is a floor covering shop near you, they probably carry heavy linoleum. It should be 1/8 inch thick or more. Ask the shop to give you their scraps, or buy a little piece. Glue it to a piece of straight smooth wood, about 5/8 or 3/4 inch thick.

Cutting the block is done about the same way as cutting a potato, except with a linoleum block, you can trace the design onto the block with carbon paper. *Remember: If you have words in your design, they have to be cut backwards in order to print frontwards.*

When the block is cut, ink it with the roller and a small amount of ink. (You can always add some if you need to.) Then lay the paper down on the inked block. There are several ways to make the block print:

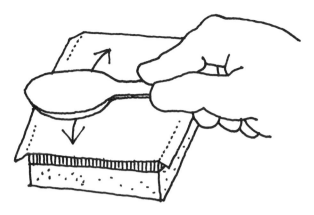

You could rub it all over with the bottom of a tablespoon. This is good for blocks that aren't too big. Be sure to press down firmly and to rub all parts of the block to transfer all the ink to the paper.

You could stomp it•with tennis shoes on. If you try this, cover the back of the paper with a piece of cardboard and step down straight so that the paper can't twist and smear the print. Gently put all your weight on the foot that is on the block, then move it to another place and repeat. Be sure to do it all over the block. Best for big blocks with large solid areas.

Things You Can Make With a Linoleum Press

You could make small posters for clubs in your neighborhood. Linoleum blocks are best for posters that fit on telephone poles. Or you could make Christmas cards or gift cards.

Ask a printer to get black cards and envelopes for you. (Maybe they have some old ones they will sell you at a low price.) Choose four of your very best card designs. Print the front only so that your customers can write their message on the inside. Sell them in sets of twenty (five of each design) with envelopes for $2.00. Package them in little sandwich bags.

Linoleum blocks are just right for printing bookplates. A bookplate is a label that you paste inside the front of a book to tell who the book belongs to. They usually have a design and the book owner's name. They can be printed on any kind of paper. You could take samples of your bookplate designs down to the bookstore or library near you and ask them to take orders. Then you can print the design and a special little block for the customer's name at once·

Expanding Your Print Shop

After you have fooled around with potato prints and lino blocks and have saved up some money, you can expand your print shop by buying a real printing press. If you live in a city and watch the classified ads under "Machinery" or "Office Equipment" or "Miscellaneous," you can sometimes find printing presses for sale. But even a small used press can cost a lot of money. And in addition you'll need other tools as well. So don't plan to get a press until you've tried the other kinds of printing first.

We know about a company whose main business is to sell printing sets to kids who want to start in the printing business. They sell presses, type and all the other things you need, even paper. You can write to them for their catalog: The Kelsey Company, Meriden, Connecticut 06450.

You didn't know that a potato was a print shop in disguise, did you?

The Sunshine Surprise-Seed Sack Makers

At the end of winter, when the snow melts and the rain stops and the sun begins to shine, everyone waits for the flowers. And when they come, it cheers everyone up. It's a very good time of year to think about flower seeds.

If you go to the library or nursery and inquire, you can probably find out what kind of hardy flowers grow easily where you live. Chances are one of the seed companies listed here will sell you flower seeds in bulk. If you buy a half-pound of each of five or six flowers that look nice together, mix a teaspoon of each and make them into little packets, you will be able to sell them to people in your town who are happy that winter is over.

Seed Catalogs

W. Atlee Burpee Co.
Riverside, California, 92502

Stokes Seeds, Inc.
Box 15 Ellicott St. Station
Buffalo, New York, 14205

RH Shumway, Seedsman
Rockford, Illinois, 61101

Be sure to choose flowers that are more or less the same height when grown, that grow at about the same rate and like the same conditions. (Don't mix flowers that love the hot sun with flowers that need deep shade.) Here are some possible combinations:

MARIGOLDS
POPPIES
NASTURTIUMS

ZINNIAS
SNAPDRAGONS
SWEET PEAS

ASTERS
ALYSSUM
GYPSOPHILA

You could call your packets "The Spring Flower Surprise Sack," or some other name. Put them into little cloth sacks that you make like the lunch bag in "The Sometimes Sew and Patchworks" section. Just make them from a smaller rectangle, about 12 inches by 5 inches. Then make a cardboard tag that you can tie to your sack by the drawstring. It might look like this:

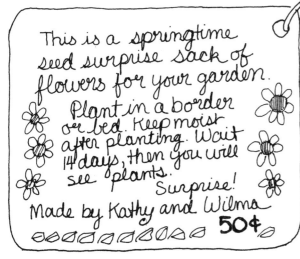

This is a springtime seed surprise sack of flowers for your garden. Plant in a border or bed. Keep moist after planting. Wait 14 days, then you will see plants. Surprise! Made by Kathy and Wilma 50¢

Penny-a-Pinch

One little five-year-old girl sold sunflower seeds for a penny-a-pinch. She'd grown the flowers the year before with the help of her mother, and she had saved all the seeds.

Free Seeds

You can pick sweet pea and nasturtium seeds in the late summer, dry them on plates or pie tins and store in a glass jar for next spring. The more you learn about flowers and saving seeds, the more profit you will enjoy. It makes sense to plant a flower seed garden.

How To Sell Your Seed Sacks

Make a little tray out of a shallow cardboard box, not too big. Fill it with sacks and make a sign for the top. Take it to the nursery, or florist, near you and ask the owner to help you sell your sacks. In return, give him or her a commission (part of the money you make).

If there is a garden club in your town, ask the members to buy your sacks. Take them to a club meeting.

Set up a little table with a display of seed sacks at any flea market or craft show. Sell them to your school friends for Mother's Day presents.

Marigolds 25 Cents Each

Here's a way to make a quarter multiply. Buy a packet of marigold seeds and plant them in a flat (a shallow wood container). Follow the planting directions on the package, set in a warm, protected spot. When your plants are three inches high, start your sale. Slice a section of marigolds out of the pan (like a piece of cake). If your plants are healthy and getting ready to set flowers, you'll probably get 25 cents each.

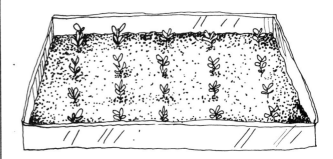

THE GLAD RAG GIRLS

or

how to get from rags to riches

First of all, this idea could be called The Glad Rag Girls *and Boys* except that doesn't sound quite as catchy. Besides, the idea comes from two sisters, Linda and Stella Allison, who had a business making and selling clothes. Now they're grown up, and Linda gave us this idea for making clothes from stuff that is worn out. This idea is really about seeing old things in a new way. Like looking at an old pair of worn-out jeans with the seat and knees worn out so you can't patch them any more—and seeing an apron.

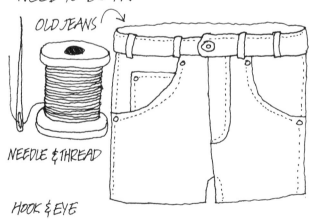

HOW TO MAKE LINDA ALLISON'S FAMOUS OLD TIRED JEANS ALL PURPOSE UTILITY APRON — READY? HERE IS WHAT YOU'LL NEED TO DO IT:

OLD JEANS

NEEDLE & THREAD

HOOK & EYE

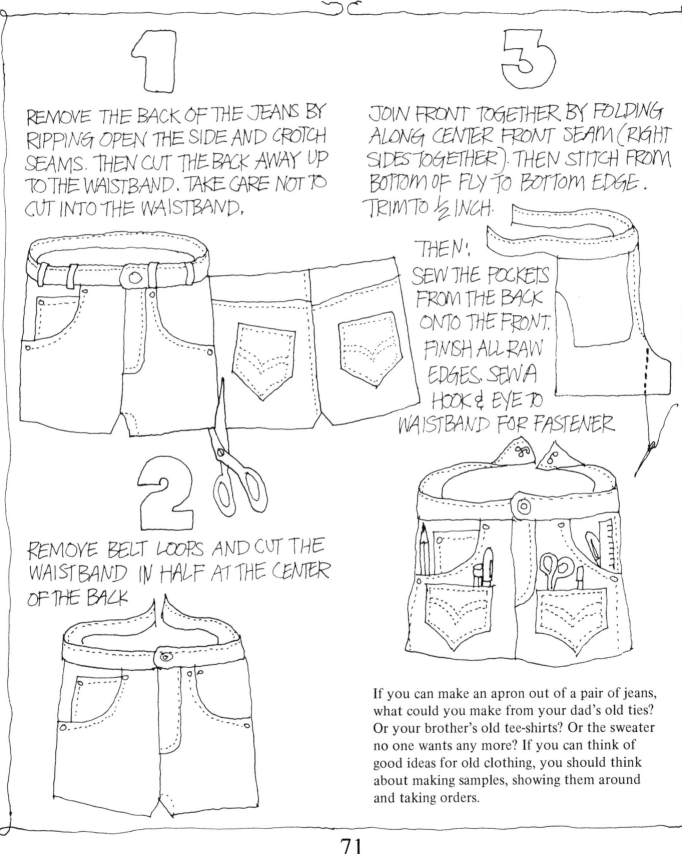

1

REMOVE THE BACK OF THE JEANS BY RIPPING OPEN THE SIDE AND CROTCH SEAMS. THEN CUT THE BACK AWAY UP TO THE WAISTBAND. TAKE CARE NOT TO CUT INTO THE WAISTBAND.

2

REMOVE BELT LOOPS AND CUT THE WAISTBAND IN HALF AT THE CENTER OF THE BACK

3

JOIN FRONT TOGETHER BY FOLDING ALONG CENTER FRONT SEAM (RIGHT SIDES TOGETHER). THEN STITCH FROM BOTTOM OF FLY TO BOTTOM EDGE. TRIM TO ½ INCH.

THEN: SEW THE POCKETS FROM THE BACK ONTO THE FRONT. FINISH ALL RAW EDGES. SEW A HOOK & EYE TO WAISTBAND FOR FASTENER

If you can make an apron out of a pair of jeans, what could you make from your dad's old ties? Or your brother's old tee-shirts? Or the sweater no one wants any more? If you can think of good ideas for old clothing, you should think about making samples, showing them around and taking orders.

THE WAX AND WICK WORKS

Inga and Berit Larsen live in San Francisco, California. Whenever during the year they get spirit (and always at Christmas!) they make candles—usually with help from their big sister, Lael. And because these girls have wonderful ideas for what looks nice, they make wonderful candles. Here is how they do it:

Supplies to have on hand:
- a block of wax (from a crafts store) or parowax (from the grocery... pretty expensive) or old broken candles (free from your neighbors)
- squares of colored wax or old crayons (to color clear wax)
- sticks for stirring
- wicks
- scissors
- several one pound coffee cans.
- a spoon (to test the color of the wax.)
- an old pan, about 12"x9"x2"
- hot pads
- an old pie plate
- a large old pan or bowl
- one quart milk cartons or one pint half & half cartons.
- frozen juice containers
- commercial candle molds (if you want to buy them)
- newspapers (lots)

Making Candles

Melt a chunk of wax in a one pound coffee can. (You can add crayons or colored wax to get the color you want.) Place coffee can in a shallow pan filled with water. Place on the stove and wait for the wax to melt. Prepare several colors at the same time (in separate cans). Wax is very flammable (catches fire easily), so handle it carefully.

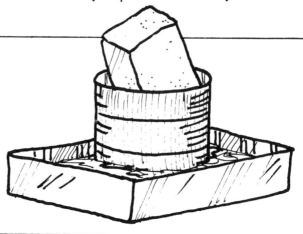

RECIPES

Rainbow Candles

Pour a little bit of colored wax into a frozen orange juice container. Wrap a wick around a pencil. Place the pencil across the top of the container so the wick will hang in the middle. As soon as the first color has hardened or set, pour on your next color. Keep adding colors until the container is full. When the final color is hard, peel off the container.

Ice Cube Candles

Cut a milk carton in half or use a pint size container. Place several ice cubes in the container. Hang a wick into the container. Quickly pour in your colored wax. Wait until the wax is hard. Pour off the water (from melted ice). Pull the container off your candle. Surprise! Your candle has holes!

Roll Ups

Pour a thin layer of wax into an old pie plate. When the wax is hard enough to lift up, slowly roll the wax into a tube shape. (If your wax sticks, try coating the pie tin with cooking oil or Mold Release, which is a special candle making product available at craft stores.) When you get half way, put a wick into the center and continue rolling. Shape the candle with your hands. Flatten the bottom so the candle will stand up.

Squishy Candles

Put cold water into a large old bowl or pan. Pour wax into the water. Shape a squishy candle with your hands, inserting the wick as you squish.

Dipped Candles

Put cold water into a large bowl. Dip a wick into wax, then dip the wick into the cold water. Straighten the wick as it collects wax. Keep dipping the wick into the wax and cold water alternately until you have a nicely shaped candle.

Finished Candles

Inge and Berit took their candles to their neighborhood center flea market and made $25. They made most of the money from the candles, but they also cleaned their rooms the day before and sold old jewelry, buttons, Cracker Jack toys, comic books and other valuable junk. Grownups bought the candles, but other kids bought the junk.

JIMMIE'S FLOATING CHRISTMAS CANDLES

Another kid we know used to make floating candles from candle-ends and crayons every Christmastime. He poured the melted wax into jello molds and muffin tins and the candles always looked beautiful floating with flowers or greens in a big bowl on the dining room table. He charged 25 cents each and took them around door to door a few days before Christmas.

This is a good way to start in the candle business because you don't have to buy wax or wicks or coloring.

Special Timers

CHUCK McCLAIN'S BIG SHOW

Out in La Canada, California (that's near Los Angeles), there is a boy who is eleven years old who is so crazy about Halloween that every year he and his friends put on a big show. Their show is a big attraction and each year it gets a little better. We asked Chuck to tell us about his show for this book and this is what he sent us. Maybe Chuck's show will give you ideas about one of your own.

THIS YEAR'S SHOW WAS IN RODNEY WHITE'S BACK YARD AND HAD A GOLD MINING THEME. THEY HAD A REAL CREEK WITH WATER, AND A SLUICE BOX, GOLD MINING PAN AND OTHER STUFF. THEY EVEN IMPORTED A DEAD TREE FROM DEVIL'S GATE DAM AND SET IT UP. LOTS OF PEOPLE CAME TO SEE THE SHOW, WHICH CHUCK CALLS "THE HALLOWEEN SCENE."

CHUCK HAD HELP WITH HIS SHOW. HERE HE IS (ON THE LEFT) WITH 2 HELPERS: BOB (CHUCK'S OLDER BROTHER) IS IN THE MIDDLE, AND RODNEY WHITE IS ON THE OTHER END. BOB IS HOLDING THEIR CREDITS BOARD. BRUCE NORQUIST ALSO HELPED.

MINER'S TENT AND GRAVE. NOTICE ALL THE MONEY AND EMPTY LIQUOR BOTTLES LYING AROUND TO MAKE IT LOOK REAL.

HERE IS BOB IN HIS COSTUME IN FRONT OF A MINER'S SHACK WHICH CHUCK AND HIS HELPERS BUILT FROM SCRATCH. NOTICE THE RESTRICTED SIGN AND OTHER MAN-MADE JUNK. THERE IS EVEN A SKULL. CAN YOU SEE IT?

Our Halloween Scene
by Chuck McClain

Our Halloween scene was made by my brother Bob, Bruce Norquist, Rodney White, and me. It was at Rodney White's house. It was in his side yard.

We had an idea of a Halloween scene about February. Then we decided to make it a gold mining town.

We started planning it in March of last year. We drove around Foothill Boulevard looking for old bottles, rusted cans, pots, dead branches, and tumbleweeds for good special effects. We went to the library and got books on ghost towns and mining camps. On Chuck's birthday we went to Knott's Berry Farm and studied their ghost town and mine. There, we bought some documents, a "Wanted" poster and a gold mining pan. We worked hard on collecting stuff all year.

We started working on it about September 22. I made a schedule of jobs for each person. The most complicated things we made were a gold mine, a miner's shack, and a river. The mine we made was in the White's cellar. We had it boarded up, then there was a stairway down to a doorway which had ripped up sheets moving because we had a fan on them. Behind the fan was a red flood light to make it look like a fire was down in the mine.

The miners shack was made of old boards and some plywood. It had one window and a wrecked door and a broken roof had a branch through it.

The river had water running through it. The water ran down under a wall, into a sluice box and into a hole. The river branched off at the sluice box and went under a walkway down into the street.

Some other things in the scene we had to make and get were a big dead tree from Devil's Gate Dam. And then we made a tent of a miner that had a candle in it. Then by the tent was a cross and a grave.

In the scene we had about seven flood lights. Bob did most of the electricity working. On the Halloween scene we had a record of sound effects playing very loud. The admission was ten cents for each person. It was a great success and it was very fun. We hope to do another one this year. It is important to get some publicity in the newspaper so people know where to go.

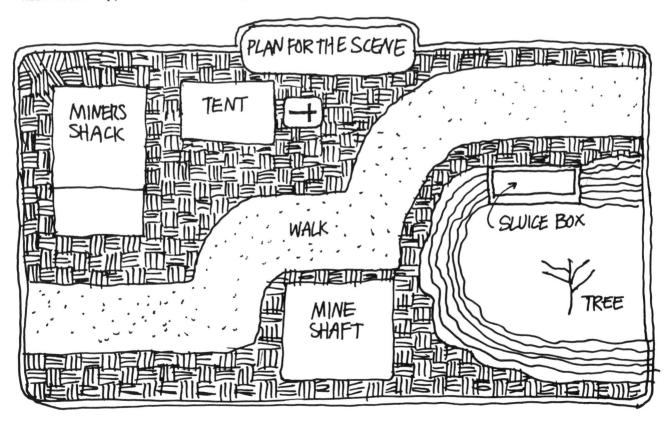

THE JACK-O'-LANTERN KIDS

You won't find a pumpkin patch in New York City. Or Chicago or any other big town. So if you live in one of those places, you can start a Halloween business that will bring a little cheer to all the people who never get to see a pumpkin patch, and might not have a jack-o'-lantern if you don't come around.

First, you'll have to make arrangements with a grocery man. Find a friendly one and explain your plan. Tell him you want to take orders for Halloween pumpkins and that you'll buy all your pumpkins from him if he gives you a special price.

Where we live, pumpkins are plentiful. They cost about 10 cents a pound. That means a five pounder goes for 50 cents. Maybe your grocer will get them for you at 8 cents a pound, and you can sell them for 10 or 15 cents a pound. The amount you make pays for your time in taking orders and delivering. After you make arrangements with the grocer, make the rounds of the neighborhood. Make yourself two display cards to take around. One should show pumpkin sizes and estimated prices. Ask your customers to pick the size they want. Tell them that you will charge by the pound.

Then show them your other card. On it, you should draw as many pumpkin faces as you can think of. (Be sure they are simple enough to actually cut in a pumpkin.) Tell your customer that for $1 extra, you will carve their pumpkin and provide a candle.

Write the order down in your order book. Be sure to put what size each person wants.

When the pumpkins arrive, get the grocer to weigh and mark each one, so you'll know how much to charge. Deliver them the afternoon of the day before Halloween at the latest. Do it the day before that if you can.

IF YOU SAVE ALL THE SEEDS FROM THE JACKS YOU CARVE, YOU CAN ROAST THEM AND TAKE THEM AROUND TO SELL TOO!

Did you know there are a lot of people who hate to buy those tacky Halloween costumes that are sold in stores for high prices? You could make homemade masks and costumes that will put a sparkle in some parent's eye and some change in your pockets. Give yourself a treat and sit down with a pencil and paper and draw designs for some weirdo, funny costumes. What did you draw? A cross-eyed, kinky-tailed cat? A fairy princess with a nose like Groucho Marx? A hobo that looks like a patchwork rag doll? A pumpkin that looks like it needs an orthodontist? Now that you've got the spooky spirit, you are ready to be a goblin garment manufacturer.

Collect materials in advance so by October 1st you are ready to begin. You'll need:

paper bags
boxes
cardboard tubes
shirt cardboard
yarn
colored paper
funny papers
markers
white glue
tape
wrapping paper
ribbons
paper plates
old sheets
inexpensive material
scissors
poster paint

Make a sample batch of costumes and take them around your neighborhood, or host a goblin fashion show in your garage before Halloween. Decorate the garage to fit the occasion. Be ready to take orders in advance. Charge $1 to $1.50 for each costume, depending on how much money it costs you to make it and how long it takes. Keep your costumes simple and funny and you'll do a terrific business. And you'll make Halloween a little bit weirder.

MARVELOUS MASKS AND COLOSSAL COSTUMES

THIS MASK IS MADE FROM A PAPER PLATE WITH HOLES FOR EYES, AND PAPER EARS AND WHISKERS GLUED ON. IT HAS HOLES PUNCHED IN THE SIDES AND A STRING RUNNING THROUGH THEM TO HOLD IT ON. IT IS PAINTED WITH POSTER PAINTS.

THIS MASK IS MADE FROM A PAPER BAG WITH THE CORNERS CLIPPED OFF AND TAPED SHUT. THERE ARE BRIGHT STRIPS OF COLORED PAPER GLUED ON FOR HAIR AND EYES; ALUMINUM FOIL FOR TEETH. CUT OUT HOLES FOR SEEING AND BREATHING.

THIS IS A PAPIER MACHÉ MASK WITH HOLES PUNCHED IN THE FRONT FOR EYES, AND SMALLER HOLES ALONG THE EDGE WITH YARN THREADED THROUGH FOR HAIR. THE MASK SHAPE IS MADE BY WRAPPING THE WET NEWSPAPER STRIPS AROUND ONE HALF OF A BLOWN-UP BALLOON. WHEN IT'S DRY, POP THE BALLOON AND PAINT THE MASK.

THIS COSTUME IS JUST AN OLD SHEET OR BIG PIECE OF MATERIAL FOLDED IN HALF, WITH A HOLE CUT IN THE CENTER FOR YOUR HEAD TO GO THROUGH. YOU COULD PAINT CRAZY DESIGNS ON IT OR SEW ON PATCHES OF BRIGHT MATERIAL. THE TAIL IS A PIECE OF ROPE, PAINTED AND SEWN ON THE BACK.

THIS CREATURE IS MADE FROM A CORRIGATED CARDBOARD BOX WITH HOLES CUT IN THE SIDES FOR ARMS AND HEAD. IT HAS CARDBOARD TUBES TAPED ON AND A SMALL CARDBOARD BOX ALSO TAPED ON WITH PECULIAR KNOBS AND DIALS PAINTED ON IT. WHAT ELSE CAN YOU THINK OF TO ADD TO THIS COSTUME?

THIS COSTUME IS MADE LIKE THE FIRST ONE, WITH THE BOTTOM CUT IN A ZIG-ZAG. IT HAS A BIG FLOPPY COLLAR MADE OF FUNNY PAPERS GLUED TOGETHER IN A BIG CIRCLE WITH A HOLE IN THE CENTER LARGE ENOUGH FOR YOUR HEAD.

Here is a fine and terrible idea. You can use your weirdest, craziest, niftiest tricks (so long as they can't hurt anyone) to scare people. You can be an architect, carpenter, artist, monster-maker and freak show organizer all in one. Then you can collect money from people who come to be scared out of their tee-shirts in your bone shaking, spine chilling, brain staggering, wailing, shrieking, hysterical, disgusting

(I can't wait.)

The idea behind this show is to take people through a darkened space and to surprise them with whatever you can think of that will be scary and weird *but in no way harmful or dangerous.* It should be dark enough so that it's scary, and so people can't get a good look at how your tricks work. But it should not be so dark that people crash about and can't find their way. (Also, if it's too dark, little kids won't go in at all, and that's bad for business.)

Most important, there must be no nails or splinters to get poked by, or greasy things that could stain clothes, or anything else that could spoil someone's scary good time. (Besides, you don't want to spend all the money you make paying to have someone's clothes cleaned or their hand stitched up, do you? I didn't think so.)

Where To Have A Spook House

Anywhere. You could do it outdoors if you can get enough tents or big huge boxes. You could make any garage into a first class spook house. Or you could do it in a basement, or even in an alley (as long as it isn't used by cars.)

There are three important design features in any good quality spook house. First, it is one way only. Traffic goes through in one direction. (That means you need an entrance *and* an exit.) Second, it should be divided into different spaces (like little rooms) where different things happen. You can do that by turning corners, or by having openings from one space into another. Third, it is darkened (but not pitch black.) Anyplace you can make those three conditions happen is a good place for a spook house.

Things That Are Good For Building Spook Houses

Old sheets and blankets. The more the better. They enclose space. They help contain sound (so people can't hear what's coming next). Sheets can be dyed spooky colors and hung in front of light bulbs to make a weird colored space. (Be sure it's okay with your parents.) Or they can be torn into strips that hang down in the face and feel icky.

Big Cardboard Boxes. The kind refrigerators come in. They make good "spook rooms." Especially if you're doing this outside. Just be sure they are anchored to the ground securely so someone doesn't accidentally knock them over.

Tents. All kinds. Pup tents. Two man tents. Family sizes.

Tarps and Parachutes. Anything your dad or big brother might have around to cover something big. (Like a car or boat.)

Big Plastic Sheets. Not the thin kind. The heavy green or black or clear stuff called "visqueen" by some people. Used like tarps.

Folding Screens, Old Doors, Door Frames. These can be used to make walls. Anything that is big enough for someone to walk under or through will work. (P.S.: Don't make doorways too small so people have to crawl or bend way over. It doesn't work.)

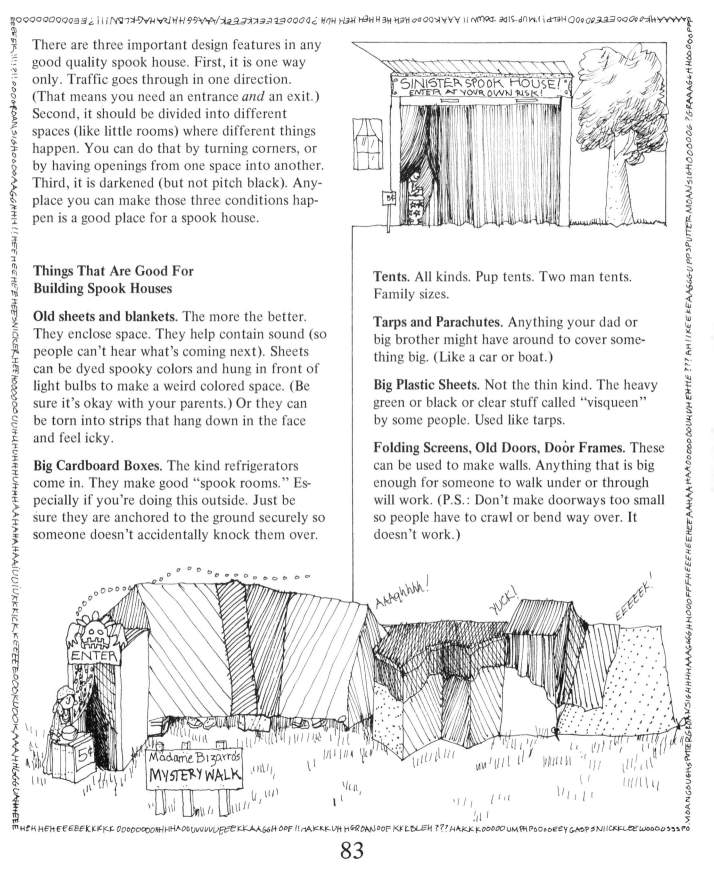

Then there are the SPOOKS! (heh, heh heh)

Things That Are *VERY SCARY*
(Can you top these?)

Spirit Lights. Get a string of those Christmas lights that blink. Only put them behind a blue or green cloth so they aren't bright. Or put blue cellophane over a flashlight, hang it from the ceiling in a corner and push it to make it swing around the room.

Ghoul Hands. Rubber gloves half full of water and tied tightly at the end.

Spiders. Rubber and black yarn ones.

Spider Webs. Hanging thread.

Ghoul Drool. Wet yarn or string.

Monster Breath. Hair dryer blowing over some smelly cheese or a can of cat food. Or use a fan.

Shrunken Heads. Paper mache heads with yarn hair with nails sticking out, hung on springs so they bob up and down.

Vampire. A kid dressed up with huge fangs who drinks from a big clear glass bottle of tomato juice. Have a fake wooden stake through his heart and have him lie in a coffin. He can rear up and take a swig when people come in.

The Gory Guts Walk. This makes a terror-ific grand finale, and works best in a garage or out-doors setup. Have the walk end with a patch of wet noodles. Yech! Get a couple of bags of the cheapest noodles you can find and cook them all. Tack one of those big plastic garbage bags to a large board so it doesn't wad up, and spread the noodles over it. Save some of them to add later on. Have one of your helpers ready with a hose or bucket of water outside the end of the spook walk to wash off gummy feet.

Sound Effects. If you have a tape recorder, here are some things you could put onto your sound effects tape to play during the walk.

Heavy Breathing. Something not too loud, but constant and a little sinister which builds up and up. If you leave it on for a while when people first come in, they will know something scary is going to happen and that will make it even scarier. Heavy breathing is good. Or you could try some kind of low dragging sound, or a heartbeat sound.

84

Weird Sounds. These are good if they sound *like* something, but not like anything exactly. Record the sound of soup bubbling—it will sound like hot lava or something worse. Fingernails scratching on blackboards are good. Dog howls slowed down or cat yowls slowed down and dog howls speeded up—either are good.

Chains To Rattle and Clank.

Crashes and Blood-curdling Screams. (Use sparingly.)

Crazy Hysterical Laughter.

Pick out sounds that go with the spooks in your spook house. Just remember that loud noises aren't necessarily the scariest.

Extra Suggestions

It's a good idea to have a little help. Let one person handle sound effects, another take money. Someone else will be needed to perform all the tricks that require people. Whoever takes money could act as guide to take the littlest kids through by the hand if they don't come with an older brother or sister.

Charge 5 or 10 cents. Not more. Don't let too many into the spook house at once. Better to have them line up outside rather than inside. And it's good advertising.

If you know all the kids in your neighborhood, you and your spook house associates should dress up in scary outfits and take the hand-written invitations around to deliver to each kid after dark. They might say something like this:

The Anytime-It-Snows Shovelers Company

WHEN WINTER COMES, THERE PROBABLY ISN'T ANYTHING YOU LIKE SO MUCH AS THE FIRST SNOW. AND THERE PROBABLY ISN'T ANYTHING YOU LIKE LESS THAN SHOVELING IT OFF THE FRONT WALK, RIGHT?

SHOVELING SNOW IS HARD WORK, AND WHEN YOU DON'T FEEL LIKE DOING IT, IT'S NO FUN. BUT HERE IS A WAY TO SET UP A BUSINESS THAT WILL MAKE THE JOB A LITTLE MORE FUN AND EARN YOU MONEY BESIDES.

Collect three friends who are willing to be your partners. Everyone has to understand that the Shovelers Company has to be dependable. Which means, when it snows all the partners have to be ready to work, no matter what.

Then make up some handouts. Take them around the neighborhood, and post them on bulletin boards wherever you can. They should say something like this

When it SNOWS, don't get STUCK.
Call this number and we will come to SHOVEL your WALK or DRIVEWAY.
☆ We bring our own tools.
☆ Your satisfaction is guaranteed. Call anytime afterschool or weekends: 675-1104. ASK FOR JIM.

Whoever belongs to the phone number on the handout is the dispatcher. He or she calls each member until they find someone who can do the work. (Even though you make a promise to work, sometimes you can't, and it isn't because you're lazy.) This way, someone is bound to be available. Distribute the jobs fairly so that everyone has a chance to work. And in heavy snows, work in teams.

The most important thing about this business is that you must work right away when it snows, because people will depend on you. Even if it means getting up early so that the lady down the street can get her car out to go to work at 8.

If you have good friends you can count on, you'll have a great winter business. Charge at least $1 for short walks, more for longer ones or driveways.

THE DOWNHOME CHRISTMAS COMPANY

This idea is for kids who especially like Christmas. It's a good way to fill up your holiday vacation with things that are guaranteed to give you the Christmas Spirit. And it will help you earn money for presents. The idea is you and some of your friends forming a kids company to bring hand-made Christmas stuff to the people in your neighborhood. Here are some things you could make.

Downhome Wreaths. Go to the first Christmas tree lot that opens in your neighborhood. Tell the manager that you want to have all the branches they trim off trees. (If the manager doesn't give them to you, they'll probably just be thrown away, so you're doing the lot a favor.) Take the branches home. On the way, pick up a spool of thin wire at the hardware store, and a skein of red yarn (the big fat kind). If there is a holly tree in your neighborhood, ask its owner to let you have some sprigs. Make your wreaths by wiring the branches together and then looping them into a circle.

Make sure the wreath is good and fat. Add branches until it is. Tie a big red bow of yarn and some holly at the top. Sell these door to door for $1 or $2. (You could make two sizes.) Or take them back to the Christmas tree lot and ask if they'd like to buy the wreaths from you. Sell the wreaths for $1, and the lot can sell them for $2.

Downhome Chimney Sox. **Lots of people don't have special socks for hanging over the fireplace Christmas Eve night. Or they need an extra for special guests. You can make big wonderful wacky ones, and even put names on them. First make a sample to take around.**

1. MAKE A PAPER PATTERN LIKE THIS →

2. CHOOSE SOME BRIGHT, HEAVY MATERIAL FROM YOUR MOM'S SCRAP BAG (IF SHE'LL LET YOU) OR FROM THE YARDAGE STORE. FOLD THE FABRIC IN HALF, SO THAT WHEN YOU CUT AROUND THE PATTERN, YOU WILL GET TWO SOCK SHAPES .... A FRONT AND BACK.

3. DECORATE THE FRONT WITH DESIGNS FROM LITTLE SCRAPS, TREES, STARS, ANGELS, LITTLE BELLS, AND YOUR NAME. YOU COULD ALSO SEW ON BUTTONS, RIBBONS, LACE, OR ANYTHING ELSE YOU CAN FIND THAT MAKES IT LOOK TERRIFIC.

4. THEN SEW THE FRONT TO THE BACK TO MAKE THE SOCK. TURN THE TWO PIECES FACE TO FACE, SEW THE EDGES, THEN TURN THE SOCK INSIDE OUT TO HIDE THE SEAM. AND LAST, SEW ON A FABRIC LOOP SO THE SOCK WILL HANG BY THE CHIMNEY.

5. THEN MAKE A TAG LIKE THIS →

Chimney Sox handmade by DAVE $1.50

Sell for $2 or more. Extra if your customers want names sewn on. Take around a sample and take orders in advance.

Too Good To Eat Ornaments. These ornaments are cookies. They look beautiful. But they taste awful. You're supposed to look at them, not eat them. You can make some to sell at Christmastime because the little ones make good tree ornaments, and the bigger ones make nice presents.

Dough
Recipe:

4 cups all-purpose flour
1 cup salt
1½ cups water, added slowly and mixed well with your hands. Knead the dough for five minutes (get a grownup friend to show you how) and then roll it out to a thickness of about 1 to 1½ inches.

To Cut
& Bake:

Use a regular cookie cutter, or a wet knife, to make your own designs. Roll up little balls of dough and stick on for noses, buttons, bumps or lumps. Bake at 350° for 45 minutes or more (depending on how thick your cookies are). Check doneness by sticking one with a pin. If it comes out clean, the cookies are done.

To hang your cookies later, stick a little wire loop through the top while they are still soft. After they have cooled (they did taste awful, didn't they!), decorate with paint or magic marker. To make them shiny, coat with lacquer after painting. Sell little ornaments for 25 cents, medium ones for 50 cents and big ones for $1.

88

Paper Snowflakes. You've probably been making these since you were five. But a lot of people don't know about these wonderful ornaments. They're easy to make, and they look nice against windows. Small ones look good on the tree.

Cut a piece of paper into an eight inch square. Fold in half. Then fold in half again. Then fold *that* in half to make a triangle. Now hold it folded and carefully cut out pieces. Be sure not to cut all the way through the shape. When you open it out, presto!—a snowflake. Each one different, just like the real things. Sell the big ones for 10 cents, the little ones (four inch square) for a nickel.

Downhome Popcorn and Cranberry Chains. The best way to do these is to have a party and get everyone to help. The only problem with that is that you sometimes eat more popcorn than you string. But if you make a batch of *buttered* popcorn to eat, then everyone will leave the plain stuff alone. (It doesn't taste nearly so good without butter.) But it does make very nice tree decorations, especially if you mix popcorn with cranberries. All you need is a needle, some heavy thread, popcorn and a lot of fingers. Sell chains for 50 cents or $1, depending on length, price of cranberries, etc. Make them at least four feet long. Put them in baggies.

old toys fixit factory

Bet right this minute there are five toys lying around your house that you got a long time ago and don't ever play with any more and wouldn't mind giving away. If everyone you know has five toys like that, how many toys does that make?

Bet if you start a toy hospital now, you can fix up old used toys slick as a whistle and sell all you can fix. There are good reasons for that. First, most used toys can be fixed up easily and look almost as good as new. Second, what is an old toy to you will be new to someone else. Third, there are a lot of grownups who are tired of buying new toys that aren't very good, for big prices. Those people will be your best customers and there are a lot of them.

If that hasn't convinced you, here are some examples of ways you can make old toys like new again. Once you start, you'll get lots of ideas of your own.

RAG DOLLS

SEW UP RIPPED SEAMS AND PATCH HOLES WITH HEART-SHAPED FABRIC. ADD YARN FOR HAIR, BUTTONS FOR EYES AND CARE- FULLY PAINT A NEW MOUTH AND ROSY CHEEKS WITH A FELT-TIPPED MARKER. MAKE A SIMPLE DRESS. TIE A RIBBON FOR HER HAIR AND ONE FOR HER DRESS.

OTHER DOLLS

REPLACE BROKEN ARMS AND LEGS BY SNAPPING THEM INTO PLACE. CLEAN THE DOLL UP WITH SOAP AND WATER. COMB HER HAIR. FIND A NICE DRESS FOR THE DOLL AND MAYBE A COLORFUL BLANKET.

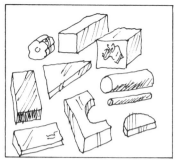

ASSORTED BLOCKS

COLLECT A LOT OF WOODEN BLOCKS. SAND ROUGH EDGES AND PAINT EACH ONE A DIFFERENT COLOR WITH ENAMEL PAINT. FIND A BOX AND COVER IT WITH WRAPPING PAPER OR PAINT. PLACE YOUR BLOCKS IN IT TO MAKE A NICE DISPLAY.

STUFFED ANIMALS

MAKE NEW ARMS AND LEGS. CUT FABRIC TO DESIRED SIZE, SHAPE. SEW THREE SIDES AND STUFF WITH COTTON, POLYESTER OR OLD RAGS. SEW NEW LEGS AND ARMS ONTO THE BODY. ADD BUTTONS FOR EYES AND CUT OUT A PIECE OF FELT AND SEW IT ON FOR A MOUTH.

How To Get Toys. Start with your friends. Tell them your idea and ask them to help by giving you their old toys. (You could also arrange to pay them 10 cents for each one when you sell it.) Ask your PTA to put a notice in the school bulletin, or put a notice at the church or on the supermarket bulletin board.

Where To Do It. Pick a place like a basement or garage where you can use paint and tools and make kind of a mess without getting in the way. An old chicken coop or garden shed fixed up would be perfect.

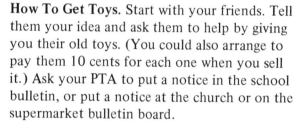

USED TOYS WANTED! WE CAN MAKE TOYS NO ONE ELSE WANTS USEFUL AGAIN. Please call Phil 473-998 or Jan, 473-8801 weekends and afterschool

When you get the toys, sort them into types. See if you can put two incomplete toys together to make one whole one.

Put the toys on shelves or in boxes until you can get to work on them. If they are in a place where you can look at them, you'll get ideas for how to fix them up while you work on something else.

SELLING WHAT YOU FIX

Don't offer your new/old toys for sale until you have a good big batch done. Get at least two or three dozen ready first. Decide in advance how much you should charge. Try to keep the prices much lower than new prices.

When the toys are ready, you could have a Big Toy Sale, or you could take them to a flea market, or you could ask the manager of a local toy store if he would like to make a special place in his store to sell Toy Hospital Toys.

Summer Timers

❈ OLD FASHIONED LEMONADE ❈

If it's hot outside and lemons aren't too expensive, maybe this is the day to think about setting up an old time lemonade stand. If you live in a place where lots of people go by and can easily stop, then you can think about people coming to *you.* If you don't live in such a place, you had better think about taking your lemonade to *them,* wherever they are. But first, you have to think about the lemonade.

People like it because it tastes good on a hot day: not too sweet, but cold, very wet and good for a dry mouth. Your first job is to make the best lemonade anyone ever tasted. And here is the recipe:

The Best Lemonade Anyone Ever Tasted

The very best lemonade is made from fresh lemons, sugar and pure, fresh water. If lemons are too expensive (don't pay more than 10 cents each), you had better use frozen lemon juice, which makes a passable, but not great, lemonade.

Mix the juice from a dozen big lemons with two cups of sugar. Put the mixture in a fruit jar with a lid and shake it up until the sugar dissolves. If you want to make pink lemonade, add a few drops of red food coloring to the mixture. Next, put two or three trays of ice cubes into a large container. A big wide-mouthed thermos jug is perfect, because it keeps the lemonade cold longest. Be sure that whatever container you use is very clean. For each batch of juice, mix twelve cups of fresh, cold water. Serve it with a ladle or a half-cup measuring cup into 7-ounce

paper cups with at least one or two ice cubes. Each batch should make thirty 7-ounce cups. If you have paid 10 cents for each lemon, you'll have to sell each cup of lemonade for 15 cents. If lemons are cheap, you could sell the lemonade for 10 cents. Here is the arithmetic.

12 lemons cost . . . . . $ 1.20
2 cups of sugar cost . . .20
30 paper cups cost 60

sell 30 cups at 15¢ each 4.50
less total cost   − 2.00

money you make $ 2.50

On a hot day, in the right location, you might be able to sell two or three batches in one afternoon.

Make A Big Sign. If you want people to stop their cars, it will help to make a sign that gives them time to stop. Or if you can get permission, ask the neighbors if you can put signs up on the way to your stand.

LEMONADE NEXT BLOCK

LEMONADE COMING UP

LEMONADE HERE

A ROLLING LEMONADE-WAGON-STAND

There are some other tricks to the lemonade trade. Make your lemonade with thin slices of lemon rind floating in it. That looks nice and also tastes good. Also, you could charge 15 cents for the first glass and 5 cents for the second (especially if lemons are not expensive). And you could sell homemade chocolate chip cookies for 5 cents each to go with the lemonade.

Remember! Making fresh homemade lemonade is something that very few people take the time to do any more. Everyone is in such a hurry. You are probably the only place for miles where a hot and thirsty traveler can get a refreshing drink of pure cold lemonade.

What is the right location? If you live in a place where people pass by *and can see your stand* in plenty of time to stop and pull over, you could try a streetside stand. But people are much more apt to stop if they are walking. And that works better on a sidewalk or downtown where people are walking anyway. Here are two kinds of stands. Take your pick, or design your own. The most important thing (aside from the lemonade) is that you be *very visible.*

A SIDEWALK STAND

The Gourd & Corn Folks

We are out standing in our field.

Here is how to turn 60 cents worth of seed that you plant in the spring into $25 worth of Thanksgiving decorations in the fall. For this business, Mother Nature is your partner. She turns seeds into beautiful ears of colored corn and wonderful lumpy white, yellow, orange and green gourds—a pretty amazing bit of work. All you have to do when she's through is offer it for sale. That's the easy part.

First go to the store and find two seed packets. The ones you want are marked *Ornamental Corn* and *Gourds Small Fruited Mixed* or similar words. Look at the pictures on the front. The corn should be crazy colors and so should the gourds.

Read the instructions on the back of the seed pack and follow them carefully. Both gourds and corn like lots of sun. Be sure to plant them in good soil where there is sun most of the day. Ask the seed person for advice if you're not sure.

Keep your garden soil moist. Both kinds of plants need water at their roots. If you plant in early May, both plants will be ready for picking about the time you go back to school. Be sure to pick them before the first frost comes. Dry the corn and gourds in a warm dry place. Hang the corn in bunches up high (where warm air circulates). Spread the gourds out on a tray or table. Don't pile them up. If you want, varnish the gourds to make them shiny.

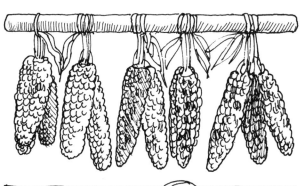

AROUND THE FIRST WEEK IN NOVEMBER, SEND OUT A POSTER OR ANNOUNCEMENT THAT YOU HAVE THANKSGIVING DECORATIONS FOR SALE. YOU COULD SELL CORN IN BUNCHES OF THREE FOR 75 CENTS, GOURDS FOR 25 OR 50 CENTS EACH, DEPENDING ON SIZE. OR YOU COULD MAKE UP ASSORTMENTS AND SELL THEM WITH COLORED LEAVES OR GREEN LEAVES AS TABLE DECORATIONS. CHARGE $2.00 OR MORE FOR ASSORTMENTS.

There most likely isn't anyone in the world who knows what a kid's birthday party should be like better than you. If you like birthdays, and if you like little kids, this might be just the right idea for you: start your own

HAPPY BIRTHDAY PARTY COMPANY

Getting started is the hardest part. The best way is with a friend, so you'll have some help. And start by doing the first one free for someone you know pretty well. Pick out some little kid you like and tell his or her mom and dad that you want to give a party as a present. If it works, and everyone has a good time, ask those parents to tell their friends about your new business. Pretty soon, word will get around.

A Party Plan

A good birthday party doesn't just *happen.* It's planned in advance. All the parts are considered and decided upon before they happen. That's important. Be sure you have a talk with parents several days before each party. To start with, let parents take care of refreshments and party favors, if any. That way you can concentrate on the other parts. Here is a sample birthday party schedule. (When you do a real one, it will be different. This one is just to give you the idea.)

Sample Birthday Schedule
(where lunch is included)

10:00	. . . . go to the birthday house and get set up
11:00	. . . . kids arrive, get their hats
11:15	. . . . active game 1
11:30	. . . . active game 2
11:45	. . . .quiet game or birthday presents
12:00	. . . eat lunch: hot dogs, chips, carrot sticks, punch, cake, ice cream
12:30	. . . . puppet show or entertainment
1:00	. . . . time to go home
1:00–1:30	. . . . clean-up time

(No one really has a birthday party by the numbers like this, but having a sense of what comes next and when helps to keep things going smoothly, and that makes it more fun for everyone.)

Getting Organized

A birthday company needs a lot of style. In a way, when you put on a party, you are putting on a grand show in which every person has a part. That's why birthday party goers get funny hats to wear. That's why maybe you and your worker-friends should wear costumes. Here are some ideas for how you could make costumes that are simple to make and comfortable to wear.

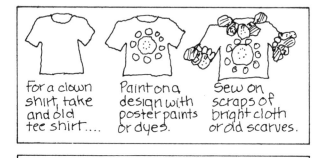

For a clown shirt, take and old tee shirt....

Paint on a design with poster paints or dyes.

Sew on scraps of bright cloth or old scarves.

MAKE A GOOFY YARN WIG. GET A BALL OF BRIGHT YARN AND SEW LOTS OF STRIPS OF IT TO THE TOP OF AN OLD STOCKING WITH THE END TIED AND CUT.

Paint your face with poster paints or rouge. (A mask is nice, but too hard to see out of.)

Lightly stuff some old gloves with newspaper and sew to the top of an old shower cap or any cap you like.

Find some suspenders to hold up the baggy pants you make from old P.J. bottoms.

With a ribbon, gather the hems of a pair of man's pajama legs and tie above your knees.

Stuff the toes of some big man's sock with cotton and sew on a couple of pompoms or clunky buttons.

BE ON THE LOOKOUT FOR SCRAPS OF MATERIAL, OLD SHEETS, SOCKS, STOCKINGS, PANTYHOSE, SHOWER CAPS, JUNK JEWELRY, YARN, COATS, BUTTONS, PAJAMAS, RIBBONS, TEE SHIRTS, PANTS, SCARVES, GLOVES, etc.

How Much To Charge. Until you've had a dry run or two and know what you're doing, charge nothing. After that, you should probably get about $8 to $10 for a two hour party for up to eight or ten kids. More if the party is especially big or complicated, less if the parents want to handle decorations as well as food.

Be sure to talk with the grownups. *Write out your plan for their party and show it to them in advance. List all the activities so they'll know what you need from them (chairs, tables, balls or other props), and so you'll know what you need to bring from home. Make sure you know whether or not there are to be presents, so you can allow time for them. (Some parents prefer parties without them.) Be sure you have the names of everyone who is coming. This discussion with the grownups is very important. Don't put it off.*

Decorations

They are pretty important, because they make any place—indoors or out—*look* like a birthday party. But each place is quite different, and you'll have to decide with the grownups who will do what. Here are some ideas for simple decorations that look nice and don't cost much.

MAKE LOTS OF PAPER CHAINS FROM THE FUNNIES. OR FROM WRAPPING PAPER TO LOOP ACROSS THE CEILING AND AT THE TOPS OF DOORWAYS. MAKE A VARIETY OF LOOP SIZES ON YOUR CHAINS.

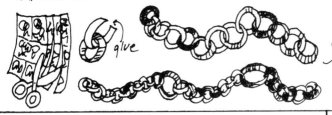

glue

BLOW UP LOTS OF BALLOONS AND STATIC-STICK THEM TO THE WALLS AND CEILING.

(RUG)

PICK A THEME FOR THE PARTY, WITH THE HELP OF THE GROWNUPS OR THE BIRTHDAY KID, THEN LET THIS FEED YOUR IMAGINATION. PICK A SEASON, OR A HOLIDAY, OR A PLACE LIKE THE ZOO OR A FARM OR THE MOON.

MAKE A FEW COLORFUL POSTERS WITH THE BIRTHDAY KID'S NAME AND NEW AGE INCLUDED ON THEM IN SOME WAY. LIKE FIVE DANCING BEARS.

10:00

Getting Ready

Get there at least a half-hour in advance. Check to be sure everything is ready. Put up any decorations you are responsible for. Set up chairs and tables for activities the way you want. Be sure to remove anything that might get broken or knocked over accidentally. Put the hats for guests where you want them.

11:00

Everybody Comes

Most little kids aren't late for birthday parties unless some grownup makes them late. So be ready on time. Be ready to keep them busy from the very start. Here are a couple of good ways to do that.

Find Your Hat

Hang all the hats from the ceiling if you can do it easily. Or put them around the room in funny places. Each hat has a name. (Have a spare blank one around just in case an extra person shows up at the last minute.) Everyone finds their hat and puts it on.

Hats You Can Make

Here are two kinds: a folded kind, and one that's made from a plain old paper bag. What's important in each is how it is made fancy. The fancier the better. Just be sure they don't get heavy or awkward, be sure they have a chin tie, and be sure each one has its owner's name on it.

HEAD-SIZE PAPER BAG ①

CUT THE FOUR CREASES OF THE BAG SO IT'S SHALLOW ENOUGH TO SIT ON A LITTLE KID'S HEAD.

TAPE THE ENDS OF THE CUTS SO THEY DON'T TEAR AND CURL UP THE ENDS AND TAPE THEM TO THE SIDES OF THE BAG.

TAPE CURLS OF PAPER TO THE CROWN OF THE BAG. USE BRIGHT WRAPPING PAPER OR ALUMINUM FOIL. PAINT ON THE KID'S NAME.

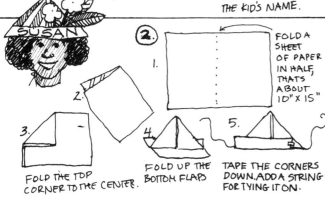

②

FOLD A SHEET OF PAPER IN HALF, THATS ABOUT 10" X 15"

1.

2.

3. FOLD THE TOP CORNER TO THE CENTER.

4. FOLD UP THE BOTTOM FLAPS

5. TAPE THE CORNERS DOWN. ADD A STRING FOR TYING IT ON.

6. DECORATE WITH PAINTS AND CUT-OUT PAPER FLOWERS OR LEAVES OR FEATHERS.

Getting Acquainted Game: Simon Sez

This familiar game is a good one to start with because it introduces you (or you and your friend) as the party clown or whatever. It's easy, fun, people can join as they arrive if they're late, and it can be any length. (You can think of lots of others.)

You be Simon and tell the kids what to do. Besides the usual things like, "Simon Sez, 'Put your hands on your head'," you could include actions with a birthday theme. Try "Simon Sez, 'Blow out the candles'," or "Point to the birthday girl," or "Eat a piece of cake."

11:15
The First Game

Plan on one or two active games and one quiet one to finish up with. This way the kids won't be too wired when they go home, or go to have refreshments or lunch. Here are two lively games that take about ten or fifteen minutes each.

FEATHER BLOW

YOU NEED ENOUGH KIDS FOR AT LEAST TWO TEAMS OF FOUR EACH. THE TEAM HOLDS HANDS IN A CIRCLE AND ONE PERSON (THE BIRTHDAY KID ON HER TEAM) STARTS BY BLOWING A FEATHER IN THE AIR. EVERYONE TRIES TO KEEP IT FLOATING AND THE TEAM WHO LASTS THE LONGEST WINS. USE A LIGHT LITTLE FEATHER, LIKE THE KIND FROM A PILLOW.

UNDER THE BRIDGE

EVERYONE STANDS IN A CIRCLE, KEEPS THEIR LEGS APART WITH THEIR FEET TOUCHING THE KID'S NEXT TO THEM. YOU NEED 8 OR 10 KIDS WITH THE BIRTHDAY KID IN THE CENTER TO START. SHE HAS A BIG RUBBER BALL AND TRIES TO ROLL IT THROUGH THE LEGS OF THE OTHER PLAYERS, THE "BRIDGES." EVERYONE TRIES TO KEEP THE BALL AWAY USING ONLY THEIR HANDS. IF SOMEONE LETS IT ROLL THROUGH THEIR LEGS, THEY'RE "IT"

11:30

The Second Game

If the first game hasn't tired everyone out, or taken too much time, play another pretty active one. Here are two more.

🥜 🥜 🥜 PEANUT RACE 🥜 🥜 🥜
SIX KIDS IS A GOOD NUMBER FOR THIS GAME.
LINE UP THREE PEANUTS IN A ROW SPREAD
OUT ACROSS THE ROOM. EACH PLAYER PICKS
UP ONE, PUTS IT IN A BASKET AT THE "GOAL",
RUNS BACK AND GETS THE NEXT ONE, PUTS IT
IN THE BASKET AND DOES THE SAME WITH THE
THIRD. THE GAME ENDS WHEN EVERYONE
HAS ALL THREE PEANUTS IN THEIR BASKETS.
FIRST DONE IS THE WINNER.

BALLOON RACE
EACH KID HAS A BALLOON AND MUST GET
IT ACROSS THE ROOM BY PATTING IT
WITH THEIR HANDS OR BLOWING IT OR
KICKING IT — ANYTHING **BUT** HOLDING
IT IN THEIR HANDS AND RUNNING WITH IT.
THE ONE TO GET TO THE FINISH FIRST IS
THE WINNER. YOU COULD PLAY THIS WITH
LITTLE TEAMS, LIKE A RELAY RACE, IF THE
KIDS ARE OLD ENOUGH TO UNDERSTAND
HOW TO DO IT.

11:45

Quiet Game (or birthday presents)

If this party has presents, this might be a good time for them. If not, try a quiet game to slow things down a bit before the refreshments or lunch time comes. Everyone sits in a circle.

I'M THINKING OF A COLOR
THE BIRTHDAY KID STARTS BY PICKING OUT
AN OBJECT IN THE ROOM AND ONLY TELLING
WHAT COLOR IT IS, SAY "RED" FOR INSTANCE.
EVERYONE TAKES TURNS GUESSING THE
RED THINGS IN THE ROOM AND THE FIRST ONE
WHO IS CORRECT GETS TO PICK THE NEXT OBJECT.

TELL A STORY
PICK OUT A STORY THAT HAS LOTS OF
CHARACTERS, AND ASSIGN ONE TO EACH
KID. THEN THEY EACH GET TO MAKE A
SPECIAL SOUND WHEN THEIR CHARACTER
IS MENTIONED AS YOU TELL THE STORY.
(DON'T FORGET PLANTS, WIND, FENCES AND
TRUCKS AS WELL AS ANIMALS AND PEOPLE.)

12:00

Lunchtime

While the kids are eating, you can be getting organized for the entertainment that follows.

12:30

The Grand Finale

Now it's time for you to put on your show. It can be a puppet show or it could be a bunch of magic tricks. Here are some ideas for a simple puppet show that little kids will like.

You could see page 108 for how to make a puppet stage, but if you want something simpler, just put a bright cloth over a card table and sit behind it so both you and the puppets are visible. Below is a magic trick to start with which introduces two puppets: a rabbit and a magician. Afterwards you could have them do silly things to you or each other, like playing tricks on you which the audience gets but you pretend not to. Or use the puppets to teach a song. Anyway, keep it short and simple, like fifteen minutes.

(1.) PUT A HAT UPSIDE-DOWN ON THE BACK EDGE OF YOUR TABLE. HAVE THE RABBIT SHOW THE AUDIENCE IT IS EMPTY.

NOW FLIP THE HAT OVER AND PUT IT JUST OVER THE BACK EDGE OF THE TABLE. NOW COMES THE TRICK! WITH YOUR FREE HAND, QUICKLY SNEAK THE MAGICIAN PUPPET, ALL ROLLED UP, INSIDE THE HAT AND THEN TURN THE HAT BACK OVER.

(3.)

NOW UNWRAP THE MAGICIAN BY HAVING THE RABBIT LOOK INSIDE THE HAT FOR HIM.

(4.) NEXT, EXPLAIN TO THE RABBIT THAT THE ONLY WAY TO GET THE MAGICIAN IS TO SAY THE MAGIC WORDS, "TWIN PINES!"

(5.) AMAZING! THIS TIME WHEN THE RABBIT REACHES INSIDE, IT PULLS OUT THE MAGICIAN. IT WOULD BE A GOOD IDEA TO HAVE THIS WORK ONLY AFTER THE AUDIENCE HAS SHOUTED THE MAGIC WORDS.

and then it's **Time To Go Home** (except for you)

1:00–1:30

Clean-up Time

Birthday parties are pretty messy affairs. Help your customer by sticking around for a half hour or so to clean up. At the very least, clean up your own things. Take down decorations. Replace moved furniture. Collect your own costumes and props. If you want to make a very big hit, help clear the table and do the dishes.

One Thing To Remember

Keep in mind that although you are putting on a show and organizing the party, you are doing it for the birthday kid. Be sure that it is *his show or her show too.* **Don't hog the party or you won't be asked back. And try to think of ways to make the birthday kid the center of attention for some of the time, at least.**

THE FANCY SHIRT FOLK

No doubt about it, this is a sure-fire for certain top grade number one idea for how to make money, plus a lot of fun. In order to start this business, you'll need some money to buy the supplies. However, once you're set up, you won't have trouble attracting customers.

WE DYE FOR YOU!
MAGIC TEE SHIRT PAINTERS
WE'LL DECORATE 1 OLD TEE SHIRT FOR $1.00
COME ONE COME ALL

The magic in this comes from Inkodyes, which you put on the tee-shirt with an eye-dropper or a brush. The colors look very blah when you first put them on. But when you put the decorated shirt in the sun to dry, the colors become bright and strong—like magic. (You can also use an oven or an iron if the sun isn't shining, but that's not so spectacular.)

Inkodyes are permanent vat dyes that do not fade. They come in all colors, and are sold in 4 ounce bottles. They cost about $1 each. You can mix the colors together to make other colors, and you can thin them with water to make them lighter and to make them go farther. Five bottles (say, red, yellow, green, blue and violet) are enough to do at least forty tee-shirts if you use them carefully.

40 shirts at $1 each equals	*$40.00*
dyes cost	*5.00*
your profit	*$35.00*

Order Inkodyes (or get the Inkodye catalog) from Screen Process Supplies Manufacturing Company, 1199 East 12th Street, Oakland, California 94606. The catalog includes a complete list of colors and supplies, as well as instructions and suggestions.

Inkodyes are especially good for making *designs*. You can also dilute them with water and use them for dying a whole tee-shirt a solid color. However, if you want to dye an entire shirt a very bright color, it would probably be much cheaper to use packaged household dye like the kind your mother or father uses to dye your best shirt red after you've spilled berry juice down your front.

The best way to start this business is to spend some time experimenting with the black tee-shirts in your own family. Decorate one for yourself, your big brother, your father, your uncle, your mother . . . anyone. Painted tee-shirts are fine for ball clubs, rock musicians, joggers, golfers, bicycle riders, polo teams, tennis players. *Everyone wears tee-shirts.* Once you've done some experimental designs on your own shirts, you're ready to open up for business.

What You'll Need

Use a garage, front porch or anywhere you can set up a work table and be near the sun. Be sure to put out a sign.

Make yourself some cardboard bodies to put the shirts on while you're working. They help keep the fabric flat, and they prevent the dye from soaking through the front and getting on the back. They also keep the shirt stretched flat while the sun is setting the color.

You'll also need a bunch of little medicine droppers for dribbling on color. They are easier to control than a brush and they use less dye. You can use a brush for small solid shapes. Try to avoid large solid shapes.

A couple of brushes, some cans or jars for water and mixing.

P.S.: You can experiment using magic markers if you can't get Inkodyes. Just remember that marking pens are not cheap either, and the colors fade pretty quickly.

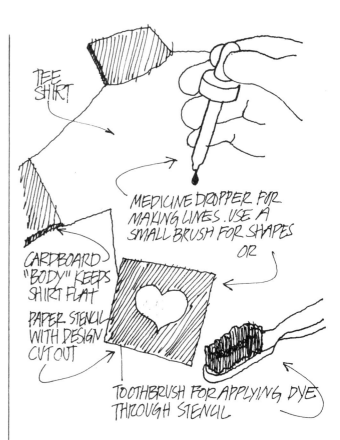

TEE SHIRT

MEDICINE DROPPER FOR MAKING LINES. USE A SMALL BRUSH FOR SHAPES OR

CARDBOARD "BODY" KEEPS SHIRT FLAT

PAPER STENCIL WITH DESIGN CUT OUT

TOOTHBRUSH FOR APPLYING DYE THROUGH STENCIL

How To Advertise

Probably the best advertisement is a fantastic looking decorated tee-shirt. Here's an idea: make three or four friends your agents. Give them a decorated shirt to wear and tell them you'll give them a 10 cent commission for each customer they bring to you. Just make sure they wear their tee-shirts. A Tee-Shirt Table makes a good booth at a flea market, art fair or bazaar, too. Anyplace there are lots of people.

Extra Ideas

You can also use Inkodyes to do tie dying. Or you could decorate a tee-shirt first, then tie dye it afterwards. Charge extra for solid colors or tie dye in addition to decoration.

If you belong to a Little League team, or a 4-H group, think about doing special tee-shirts for each member with the name of the club or team on the back. Then think about how many other clubs you could do the same thing for.

THE YARD PEOPLE

A yard person is someone who makes money by taking care of yards. Back yards, front yards, any yards. Mostly in the summertime. Yard people do things like mowing lawns, or watering, or pulling weeds, or trimming hedges or shrubs. Sometimes yard people get to pick fruit, and sometimes they build or mend fences, or paint lawn furniture. Mostly they do what their customers ask of them.

Summertime isn't the only time that yard people do their work. In the fall they rake leaves or turn the compost pile. In the winter they might cut fire wood or shovel snow. But summertime is a good time to start a yard people business if you have a mind to.

One of the reasons that summer is a good time is because that is the time to take care of yards while people are off on their vacations.

YARDSITTERS
We'll: water your grass
mow your lawn
pull your weeds
While you enjoy your
VACATION
Call Rhonda and Dave
827-8830

THE SATURDAY SOMETIMES PUPPET PALACE

If you are one of those kids who likes shows a whole lot, and if there are lots of *little kids* in the neighborhood, here is an idea you could think about. You could start a Saturday puppet theater in your garage, backyard or in a park near your house. Not every Saturday. Just sometimes. All you need are puppets, a theater and a story. And here are some ideas for all three!

We're talking about hand puppets, the kind you put on like a funny glove and move when you wiggle your fingers. You can make them easily from odds and ends around the house. Over on page 109 is a play called "Where's My Socko?". It would be just right for a puppet palace (unless you write your own play). And here is how to make the puppets for the play.

THE PUPPETS

HERE ARE BINGO AND SOCKO. THEY ARE THE GOOD GUYS. THEY ARE BOTH MADE OF SOCKS AND HAVE YARN SEWN ON TOP FOR HAIR AND BIG LUMPY BUTTONS FOR EYES. THE HANDS NEXT TO THEM SHOW HOW THEY FIT ON YOUR HANDS.

CUT HOLES IN THE **SOCKO** SOCK FOR YOUR FINGER AND THUMB. SEW ON TWO FINGERS FROM AN OLD GLOVE FOR ARMS. STUFF A THIRD FINGER WITH COTTON AND SEW IT ON FOR A NOSE.

SEW A RED CLOTH PATCH JUST ABOVE THE MIDDLE OF THE **BINGO** SOCK FOR A MOUTH.

BONGO AND TANGO ARE TWO DEEP-SPACE MONSTERS. THEY ARE MADE FROM CUT-OFF PANT LEGS.

BONGO HAS A PLASTIC COTTAGE CHEESE TUB TOP SEWN INTO ONE END OF HIS LEG FOR A MOUTH AND PAINTED PING-PONG BALL EYES. HIS SCALES ARE CARDBOARD.

SEW **TANGO'S** TOP END SHUT, WITH CARDBOARD TEETH STICKING OUT. HIS PAPER EYES ARE TAPED TO SPRINGS SEWN TO HIS HEAD, AND HIS SEVERAL ARMS ARE TOILET PAPER TUBES. YOUR FINGERS COULD FIT THROUGH ONE OR TWO TUBES.

KONGO!! THE SOCK-EATING DRAGON WORN BY AN ENTIRE KID! HIS HEAD IS A PILLOW CASE AND HIS BODY IS AN OLD SHEET. PUT A BOX UNDERNEATH LIKE THIS→

CAREFULLY SEW THE BOTTOMS OF TWO EGG CARTONS TO THE PILLOW CASE FOR A MOUTH.
THE SOCK GRABBERS ARE KITCHEN TONGS.
IMPORTANT ⇨ KONGO'S BARE FEET MUST SHOW UNDER THE COSTUME —

TIE THE CORNERS WITH RIBBONS OR EMPTY BALLOONS.

MAKE BIG WEIRD EYES FROM PAPER, OR PAINT THEM ON. BE SURE YOUR EYE HOLES ARE BIG ENOUGH AND IN THE RIGHT PLACE.

PAINT THE SHEET IN CRAZY COLORS. GLUE A LONG, RED BALLOON IN THE MOUTH FOR A TONGUE

TIE BALLOONS ON A STRING FOR A TAIL.

○○○○ MAKING THE PUPPET PALACE ○○○○

A puppet palace can be a cardboard box, some chairs and a blanket, or anything that shows the puppets and hides the puppeteer (that's you). Here is a design for one that is easy to make from a big cardboard box (the kind that mattresses or refrigerators or other big things come in). Ask around at a furniture store for the box. When you get it, here's what you do:

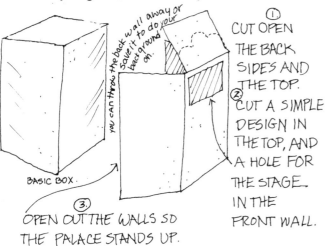

BASIC BOX.

you can throw the back wall away or save it to do your background on.

① CUT OPEN THE BACK SIDES AND THE TOP.
② CUT A SIMPLE DESIGN IN THE TOP, AND A HOLE FOR THE STAGE IN THE FRONT WALL.
③ OPEN OUT THE WALLS SO THE PALACE STANDS UP.

④ TACK A WIRE TO THE BACK CORNERS TO KEEP YOUR PALACE FROM OPENING MORE THAN YOU WANT.
⑤ TACK ANOTHER WIRE ABOUT ONE FOOT FROM THE FRONT AND HANG UP YOUR BACKGROUND WITH CLOTHES PINS. (BE SURE YOUR BACKGROUND IS BIGGER THAN THE STAGE.)
⑥ PAINT YOUR PALACE, OR GLUE ON PICTURES OR BOTH.
⑦ HAVE BOXES FOR PROPS TAPED TO THE TWO WALLS TO ADD SUPPORT TO YOUR PALACE.

The Play

This is the story that goes with Socko, Bingo, Tango, Bongo and Kongo. You probably have ideas for your own stories that are just as good as this one. But if you like this story, try it out on your little sister or brother. Later on, you can change it, or write your own.

Where's My Socko?

A PLAY FOR THE SATURDAY SOMETIMES PUPPET PALACE, BY JAMIE JOBB

Cast of Characters

Socko and **Bingo** — the two good guys.

Bongo and **Tango** — the two deep-space monsters.

Kongo! — the sensational deep-space sock-eating dragon! The deepest deep-space dragon of them all.

Props

2 sleeping bags. Use the sleeves from a worn-out furry sweater.

1 tree. Use a whisk broom or the branch from a real tree. Make sure it has a handle long enough for you to shake it backstage without your hand showing.

1 space ship. Made out of a paper towel roll and cardboard. Decorate it.

1 gas can. Made out of a pill bottle and a pipe cleaner. Make a sign that says "GAS".

1 city background. Cut out pictures of buildings and other tall things from a magazine. Paste them on a piece of cardboard big enough to fill the background behind the puppets.

1 Soupiter background. Make another background out of weird magazine pictures. Make it strange.

ACT 1

It is night. A city is in the background. A tree is in the foreground. The moon is in the sky. Socko and Bingo are in the park. Bingo is almost asleep in his sleeping bag. But Socko is a little scared. He has his sleeping bag in his mouth. He is trying to straighten it out. He is also trying to sing.

SOCKO: *(mouth full)* Muuuuuggggle . . . pwaaaa . . . (or something).

BINGO: Will you be quiet! We have to blast off for Soupiter first thing in the morning.

Socko drops his sleeping bag. Now he can talk.

SOCKO: But why do we have to spend the night here in the park?

BINGO: Because! It's the last time we'll see trees and grass and the city and the park for a whole 298 years!

SOCKO: Wow! 298 years! I'll be older than a grownup by then!

Bingo is almost asleep. Socko is not sleepy at all. He looks around the park.

BINGO: *(very tired)* Good night, Socko . . . (He yawns.)

SOCKO: Good night, Bingo . . . .

Bingo is quickly asleep and snoring. Suddenly there is a strange noise. The tree shakes. Bingo does not wake up.

SOCKO: *(screaming)* Bingo!!!

Bingo rolls over in his sleeping bag, but does not wake up. Everything is quiet for a bit. Socko goes over to the tree and tries to move it. He can't. Behind him, Bongo the deep-space monster comes in. Socko suddenly sees the monster and starts shaking. The tree shakes too.

SOCKO: Who . . . are . . . y-y-you?

Bongo the monster starts dancing around and singing. Suddenly he stops.

BONGO: *(deep voice)* I am Bongo!

Another deep-space monster jumps on stage. It is Tango. He dances wildly. Then he stops.

SOCKO: And who are . . . y-y-you?

TANGO: *(high voice)* I am Tango!

Bongo and Tango do a monster dance together. Socko hides behind a tree. The monsters stop.

BONGO &
TANGO: *(together)* We are from Soupiter. We have a warning. Don't go to Soupiter. You won't be able to get back. Soupiter is out of gas.

TANGO: *(speaks by himself)* And Kongo is out of socks. Don't go to Soupiter.

Bongo and Tango run off stage quickly. It is very quiet again. Socko comes out from behind the tree. He is still scared. He goes over to sleeping Bingo and starts to shake him.

SOCKO: Bingo! Bingo! Wake up! Something awful happened.

Bingo gets up slowly. He is still wearing his sleeping bag. And he is angry.

BINGO: AAArrrggg . . . What's going on, Socko?

SOCKO: *(very excited)* Bingo! Bingo! Two monsters came here and danced all around and said we shouldn't go to Soupiter tomorrow. We'll run out of gas . . . .

BINGO: Is that what you woke me up for? To tell me about your dreams?

Bingo picks up Socko's sleeping bag and dumps it on Socko's head. Then Bingo lies back down to sleep. Socko stands there, dumb.

BINGO: Go back to sleep now and don't wake me up again. We have all the gas we need.

SOCKO: But Bingo . . .

BINGO: Be QUIET!

Bingo rolls over and goes back to sleep, snoring. Socko still has his sleeping bag on his head.

SOCKO: *(whispering)* We'll find out in the morning. . . .

The curtain comes down.

ACT 2

Soupiter is in the background. It is a very strange planet. Socko and Bingo's space ship is in front. It is daytime. Two suns shine in the sky.

Socko and Bingo come in. Socko is carrying a gas can in his mouth.

BINGO:　I don't see any gas stations open . . . .

SOCKO:　*(can in his mouth)* MMMMmmmmbble fluuummmm *(or something)*.

Socko spits out the gas can and starts again.

SOCKO:　I told you. Soupiter is out of gas!

BINGO:　That's what *you* think. I'll find gas here. Or my name isn't Bingo Mono-poly. You wait here.

Bingo picks up the gas can and goes off.

SOCKO:　*(looking around)* Soupiter is out of gas, out of air, out of water, out of trees, out of parks, out of people, out of *everything.*

Suddenly the most monstrous deep-space dragon Kongo! comes in front of the stage. At first Socko doesn't see him. Kongo looks like he is hungry. He has big teeth.

SOCKO:　Where does he think he'll find gas? *(He notices Kongo now.)* . . . HUH?

KONGO:　*(very scary)* I am Kongo!!! I am hungry!!!

SOCKO:　*(scared)* Ah . . . It's not p-p-polite to . . . b-b-bite. Besides I'm j-j-just a s-s-stranger.

KONGO:　What do you want on Soupiter?

SOCKO:　We just w-w-want some g-g-gas . . . so we can g-g-go h-h-home . . . .

KONGO:　*(looks angry)* We told you! Soupiter is OUT OF GAS! But that's okay. I'm out of socks too. And it looks like you'll fit just fine.

Look out! Kongo bites into Socko and pulls the very puppet right off your hand. Your hand looks around . . . and wonders why everything looks so weird. It makes a fist and shakes. It is scared.

KONGO:　Ha! Ha! Ha! So long, Socko! Ha!

The empty hand goes over to the space ship and hides. Bingo returns. At first he doesn't notice Kongo.

BINGO:　No gas over there. Hey! Who are you?

KONGO:　I am Kongo!!!

When Kongo says this, he shakes his arm and Socko's empty puppet sock falls out of Kongo's hand.

BINGO:　Oh, no! What have you done to my Socko!

KONGO:　You can always get another one.

BINGO:　You don't understand. We're a real pair! *(crying)* Oh, I'll never find another Socko! Ah . . .

The hand that used to be Socko comes over and bumps Bingo.

BINGO:　What . . . are you?

The hand can't talk. It tries to make sense in sign language.

KONGO:　I'll show you who he is.

Kongo bites down on Bingo and pulls that puppet off your other hand. Now both hands are there without puppets on them. The hands both are scared and grab onto each other. They hide behind the space ship.

KONGO: You can get gas on Mupiter. They always have it. You better go now.

The hands that were Socko and Bingo pick up the space ship and blast off with a big BOOM!

Meanwhile Kongo sits down and tries to put the Socko and Bingo puppets on his bare feet. Finally he gets them on.

KONGO: *(to audience)* We told them we were out of socks. But they didn't believe us.

He leaves with Socko and Bingo puppets flopping on his feet.

The End

OOOO PUTTING ON THE SHOW OOOO

After you have tried out the show a couple of times, and you think it is ready for the public, you need to let people know about it. Saturday afternoon is a good time. So on Saturday morning, let people know that later there will be a puppet show. Here are some publicity ideas.

Put up a big poster near the place you will have the show. On your garage door, in the park or wherever. Be sure to put the name of the play, the time and place and admission price.

Make some little posters. Put them up at the library, or the playground or at the market. Think of places where people with little kids are apt to go on Saturday morning (maybe the laundromat?).

Charging Admission. *At first, don't charge more than 10 cents for kids and 25 cents for grown-ups. Later on, when you have more experience and are writing your own stories (or making puppet plays from a fairy tale or other stories) you can charge more.*

112

For your FRESH BAIT SHOP, here's how to catch worms, or
NIGHTCRAWLERS

This is all about how to make money by selling worms to fishermen for bait. It's not for people who don't like crawly things, and it's not for people who live in places where there isn't any dirt or any place to fish. Worms live in the ground so you've got to have dirt. And they won't be any good for bait if there isn't any fishing where you live. So if you have fish, dirt and worms nearby, you can be in business.

After dark, go out in your backyard with a flashlight and a covered box, and look on the ground and under rocks.

IF IT HAS RAINED THAT DAY, OR THE YARD IS WET FROM BEING WATERED, YOU'LL PROBABLY HAVE BETTER LUCK.

TO SAVE YOUR WORMS FOR THE NEXT DAY — OR LATER — PUT THEM IN THE REFRIGERATOR (OR FREEZER IF YOU WANT TO KEEP THEM LONGER) AND BE SURE THE TOP IS TIED ON THE BOX, WITH A FEW LITTLE HOLES PUNCHED IN IT.

Getting the Worm Word Out

You could start by telling people you know who fish, and asking them to spread the word. Put a sign up in your front yard or a window, and a couple of signs on the side of a nearby main street.

Ask your neighbors if it's okay to look in their backyards. Be sure to say when you'll be there.

Nightcrawlers for SALE!
231 K-St.

Be sure you have waxed paper, rubber-bands, and cans or jars to keep your customers' worms in.

Charge about 25¢ for a dozen, or less if you can get a good supply

The City Mouse Bird Feeders!

If you live in a city, chances are there are lots of birds living there, too. Also, chances are the birds and the people don't know much about each other. (I'm actually not sure about the birds, but I *know* that the people don't know much about their bird neighbors.) That's where you come in, making and selling bird feeders for city people, plus the bird seed to go with them. You can help the birds. And you'll be doing your neighbors a favor, too. They'll thank you once they know how good it is to get to know their local birds. Everyone needs a bird friend or two.

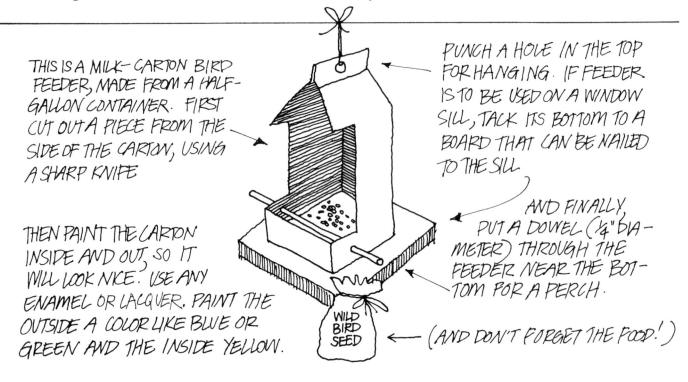

THIS IS A MILK-CARTON BIRD FEEDER, MADE FROM A HALF-GALLON CONTAINER. FIRST CUT OUT A PIECE FROM THE SIDE OF THE CARTON, USING A SHARP KNIFE

THEN PAINT THE CARTON INSIDE AND OUT, SO IT WILL LOOK NICE. USE ANY ENAMEL OR LACQUER. PAINT THE OUTSIDE A COLOR LIKE BLUE OR GREEN AND THE INSIDE YELLOW.

PUNCH A HOLE IN THE TOP FOR HANGING. IF FEEDER IS TO BE USED ON A WINDOW SILL, TACK ITS BOTTOM TO A BOARD THAT CAN BE NAILED TO THE SILL

AND FINALLY, PUT A DOWEL (¼" DIAMETER) THROUGH THE FEEDER NEAR THE BOTTOM FOR A PERCH.

WILD BIRD SEED

(AND DON'T FORGET THE FOOD!)

In fact, that could be your motto: *Everyone needs a bird friend or two.* Most birds, even those that live in cities, have places called territories where they more or less hang out. Bird places can be one tree, or a block or two or more, depending on the kind of bird and how many there are. If you have a bird feeder near a window, and keep it filled with food and away from neighborhood cats, you will soon begin to distinguish two types of bird visitors: regulars and drop-ins. What species of each, and how many, depend mostly on where you live. Some areas have more species than others. If you have a guidebook to regional birds, you'll soon learn the names and habits of all your visitors.

HERE ARE SOME BIRDS YOU MIGHT SEE:

SWALLOW

WOOD-PECKER

STELLAR JAY

OREGON JUNCO

MOCKING BIRD

HUMMINGBIRD

BLACKBIRD

BROWN TOWHEE

 YOUR LIBRARY WILL HAVE BOOKS ON HOW TO MAKE MORE ELABORATE FEEDERS OUT OF WOOD AFTER YOU HAVE TRIED THIS ONE.

On the opposite page is the design for a bird feeder that you could make at home with very ordinary tools. (If you have no experience with tools, you may have to ask a grownup to help you.)

Make one sample bird feeder. Try it out at home and get to know your own birds first. It may take several weeks for the birds to find it, so be patient. Then, take a sample feeder around the neighborhood with a little handout you can leave behind. Your handout should say something like this:

> JOIN THE
> CITY MOUSE BIRD FEEDERS
>
> IT COSTS ONLY $2 TO JOIN. YOU GET A BIRDFEEDER AND A SACK OF WILD BIRDSEED TOO. ALSO A LIST OF THE BIRDS YOU MIGHT EXPECT TO SEE AT YOUR NEW BIRDFEEDER. CALL 774-4358 AND ASK FOR ESTHER.
>
> "EVERYONE NEEDS A BIRD FRIEND OR TWO"

If you get a bunch of customers for your bird feeders, check back with each one later and ask them if they would like you to bring them bird seed and birdnews once every week or two. Ask each person to tell you what birds they saw. Write up the news and make a copy for each customer. You can buy wild bird seed in bulk from a pet supply house, and divide it into your own smaller sacks—enough for one bird feeder for a week or two. Charge 50 cents to $1 for each supply of seed and be sure to include with it a copy of your birdnews.

It won't be long until your whole neighborhood will be full of bird watchers and happy birds.

THE SUPER SANDWICH MAKERS

There are a couple of things you should know about this idea before you read any further. To do it, you have to like to *eat* sandwiches. Not crummy sandwiches, with squishy white bread and limp lunch meat. I mean big bulging healthy munchy toothsome sandwiches that taste like something real. You've got to like to *eat* sandwiches like that in order to know how to *make* them. Next, you have to have a good place to sell your sandwiches, and be pretty certain you can do it, because in order to start this business you'll need help from your mother or father, or some other adult, and maybe a loan.

It will take about $5 worth of supplies to make twenty sandwiches like the ones described below. So you need to have $5 to get started in business. (That's called capital.) *But if you sell twenty super sandwiches for $1 each, you will get your $5 back and have $15 left over. Not bad for a morning's work.*

How to start this business if you don't have $5. Go to the neighborhood market, and tell the owner your plan. Tell them you want to sweep, or wash windows, or deliver groceries, or go around the neighborhood collecting stray grocery carts to raise $5 so you can spend it at their store. If they are any kind of business person,

they will understand what you're trying to do and help you. (They might even let you sell sandwiches at their store.) Or you could tell your mom or dad or another adult that you'll wash windows, mow lawns, etc., to raise the money. Or, as a last resort, take out a loan. Just remember, if you borrow $5 to start your business, you should be prepared to pay *interest* on the money. That means that when you pay it back, you pay back the $5 plus something extra for the use of the money.

Now, about sandwiches. Here are four super sandwich recipes. (Don't try to make too many kinds. Three or four are plenty. Try these, and add your own recipes until you find out which ones sell best.)

THE CHEESE SPECIAL

FOR EACH SANDWICH, GRATE A BIG PORTION OF CHEDDAR CHEESE. THEN SPREAD A LOT OF MAYONNAISE ON 2 SLICES OF WHOLE WHEAT BREAD.

HEAP ON THE CHEESE, THEN ADD THIN SLICES OF TOMATO, AVOCADO AND RED ONION.

(THEY'LL SAY "GIMME CHEESE, PLEASE!")

THE EGG SALAD WONDER

HARD BOIL ONE EGG FOR EACH SANDWICH. THEN REMOVE THE SHELL AND MASH WITH A FORK. MIX WITH LOTS OF MAYONNAISE, CHOPPED ALMONDS AND GREEN ONION SLICES.

SPREAD THICKLY ON RYE BREAD.

FAR OUT

THE CREAM CHEESE SWEET

MASH A LARGE PACKAGE OF CREAM CHEESE UNTIL IT IS VERY SMOOTH. ADD CHOPPED DRIED APRICOTS, RAISINS OR OTHER DRIED FRUIT. SPREAD IT ON RAISIN BREAD. MAKES ABOUT 4 SANDWICHES. (YOU CAN CUT THESE INTO HALVES AND SELL EACH FOR 50¢)

THE COTTAGE CHEESE CRUNCH

MIX A 16 OUNCE CARTON OF COTTAGE CHEESE WITH A HANDFUL OF SHELLED & SALTED SUNFLOWER SEEDS, AND A HALF A CUP OF CUCUMBERS CHOPPED INTO TINY PIECES. SPREAD ON WHOLE WHEAT BREAD. ADD SOME SALT, THIN ONION SLICES AND ALFALFA SPROUTS. MAKES 6.

Get a grownup friend to let you use a kitchen with a big table or counter. Arrange things so that you can put all the cheeses together at once, then all the eggs, etc. If you have a helper, you can divide up the work.

Make your sandwiches right after breakfast each day. If you want, do the slicing and hard-boiled-egging and other getting-ready stuff the night before. But *never* make the sandwiches the night before.

Wrap the sandwiches in waxed paper or clear plastic and tie them with colored yarn. The yarn looks nice and you can use the colors to help you tell egg from cheese.

Charge 75 cents to $1 per sandwich. Make a sign to go with your sandwiches. The sign should say something like this:

HAVE A
SUPER SANDWICH
Made fresh this morning in my mom's kitchen by Morris and Martha. Only
$ 1.00 each
(YOU'LL WISH YOU'D BOUGHT TWO!)

Where To Sell Sandwiches

If you can get permission, go around to offices near you. Especially go to places where people would go out and buy their lunch anyway. (Tell them it's such a nice day they ought to eat a sandwich outdoors.) Sandwiches aren't much good in the afternoon, so be sure to start in plenty of time. Ten o'clock isn't too early. Until you have established a number of places to go, start with fewer sandwiches. Better to sell out than to have leftovers. And begin with Monday-Wednesday-Friday, rather than every day. (You need some days in between to go swimming.)

TOBY WILSON'S BERRY BUSINESS

If you live in a place where wild berries grow, you're in business as soon as they get ripe. Many folks are too lazy to get out with a pail and pick. They don't know how nice it is to stand out in the sun listening for frogs or crickets and watching for birds or rabbits while you pick. And they don't know how good a ripe berry tastes when you sample one warm from the bush. If they did, they'd all be there.

Toby Wilson (brother of Jon) used to pick blueberries. He'd pick them by the bucket, then package them up in baggies and sell them to neighbors for 25 cents a bag.

You could pick blueberries (for muffins, pies, on top of breakfast cereal), huckleberries, blackberries, boysenberries. Any kind that grows in a place where it's okay to pick. (Don't be like crazy Arthur Centurion who picked someone's flowers right out of their garden, then sold them to all the neighbors!) Be sure you have permission if they grow on the neighbor's property.

HOW TO MAKE A FREEZER BERRY BAG

TOBY WILSON HAD A SURE-FIRE METHOD FOR PUTTING HIS BERRIES IN BAGS.

HE'D USE PLASTIC FREEZER BAGS, SUCK THE AIR OUT OF EACH ONE WITH A STRAW, THEN TIE THE TOP WITH A TWISTY. THAT PRESERVES THEM BETTER IN THE FREEZER AND MAKES A NICE, NEAT PACKAGE TO SELL.

THE BIG BLOCK FAIR

This neighborhood event could be the grand finale of a summer spent making good cents. Here's a way to celebrate the many ways and means of having fun, making money and getting to know all the folks in your neighborhood.

You and a few friends can be the organizers of this event. Talk to your friends about the idea; talk to your parents. When everyone is excited about the idea, it's time to set the date, place and time. If you plan to have it on your block, you might have to discuss closing the street with your local police department or town council. They'll most likely get into the community spirit and say yes.

Set up an advertising committee of two or three kids. Make banners, posters and flyers to hang and pass around the neighborhood or nearby neighborhoods a couple of weeks before the fair. Another good idea is to select a symbol or logo for the fair. Example: if the fair is being held on Oak Avenue, then an oak leaf would make a good symbol. Put this symbol on all your posters and also make name tags for the fair workers. This kind of advertisement will help people remember the fair and if they have questions they will ask you about it.

The fair organizers will have to decide how many booths and events to have. Make sure to have a lot of variety. You'll need one person that signs up people who want to have booths. Draw a diagram of the block and chart each booth's (or table's) position and put that person's name in that space. Assign a number so there will be no confusion on fair day. On the morning of the fair, someone should take a piece of chalk and mark the numbers on the pavement so when the people arrive they know exactly where to go. Each person who participates should make their own booth or bring their own table.

119

SOME IDEAS FOR THE FAIR

SET UP AN EASEL AND DO QUICKY PORTRAITS WITH FELT-TIPPED MARKERS. CHARGE 25¢ A DRAWING.

MAKE A SANDWICH BOARD SIGN THAT SAYS

I LOVE TO BABYSIT call LAEL 383-5768

GARDEN of DELIGHT

SET UP A GARDEN OF DELIGHT. SELL PLANTS, PACKETS OF SEED, FRESH FLOWERS AND SMALL POTS OF FRAGRANT HERBS.

PRESENT A THREE PENNY OPERA. TRAIN YOUR DOG TO HOWL (HOUND DOGS DO THIS BEST); HOWL WITH HIM. WEAR TATTERED CLOTHES AND TIE A BANDANA AROUND YOUR DOG'S NECK. THIS SPECTACLE WILL BE WORTH THREE PENNIES, MAYBE MORE.

DISPLAY AND SELL ALL THE CRAFT ITEMS YOU'VE BEEN MAKING ALL SUMMER: CANDLES, PRINTED CARDS, STUFFED ANIMALS, PATCHWORK APRONS OR MACRAME NECKLACES.

PATCHWORK PURSES

FORM A JUG OR KAZOO BAND. WEAR FUNNY GET-UPS. PASS A HAT AFTER EACH PERFORMANCE.

Better practice ahead of time or be prepared to have dog washer's hands.

BRING A SCALE TO YOUR BOOTH. CHARGE DOG OWNERS 15¢ AND TRY TO GUESS THE WEIGHT OF THEIR DOGS. IF YOU GUESS WITHIN 5 POUNDS EITHER WAY OF THE CORRECT WEIGHT, YOU KEEP THE 15¢. IF YOU LOSE, THEN YOU GIVE THE OWNER A COUPON FOR A FREE DOG WASH.

CHARGE 10¢ FOR THE BOBBING FOR APPLES GAME. THE PRIZE FOR WINNING IS A JUICY APPLE TO EAT. NON-WINNERS GET A CLEAN FACE.

PUT UP A SMALL TENT AND DRESS UP IN YOUR BATHROBE WITH A TURBAN AROUND YOUR HEAD. ADD A CRYSTAL BALL OR TEA LEAVES AND ACT VERY MYSTERIOUS. CALL YOURSELF CASSANDRA THE GREAT! EVERYONE LOVES TO HEAR THEIR FORTUNE. MAKE UP SOME WHOPPERS!

121

PRESENT A ROLLICKING PUPPET SHOW WITH PUPPETS YOU'VE MADE. MAKE A SIMPLE THEATER OUT OF A LARGE CARDBOARD BOX. CHARGE 10¢ FOR ADMISSION. IF YOU MAKE ALOT OF PUPPETS YOU COULD SELL THEM AFTER THE SHOW FOR 50¢ — $1.00

BE THE OFFICIAL FLOWER KID AND PAINT TINY, DELICATE FLOWERS ON CHEEKS OR TIPS OF NOSES FOR 5¢ EACH. BE SURE AND USE WASHABLE PAINT.

BE THE GOOD FOOD KID.....

BRING HOMEMADE SANDWICHES, COOKIES AND LEMONADE. YOU'LL HAVE THE BUSIEST BOOTH AT THE FAIR!

DECORATE A CARDBOARD BOX AND MAKE RAFFLE TICKETS. SELL THE TICKETS FOR 10¢ EACH. THE WINNER OF THIS EVENT GETS TWO HOURS OF FREE BABYSITTING. YOU MIGHT COME OUT AHEAD ON THIS AND YOU'LL CERTAINLY GET ALOT OF FREE ADVERTISEMENT FOR YOUR SERVICE. FROM YOU.

SPECIAL USED MUSIC

GATHER UP ALL THE GOOD JUNK YOU'VE BEEN COLLECTING AND SET UP A FLEA MARKET STALL. SELL REPAIRED TOYS, RECORDS, BOOKS AND EUCALYPTUS POD FLEA COLLARS.

122

You and Your Money

The last few pages of this book look quite different from the rest. There are very few drawings, and no ideas for making money. These pages have information about some things that are not quite so much fun, but very important anyway.

These pages talk about what happens to your money (and to you) once you have earned it. There is information here about banks and savings and loan associations, about income tax and a little card called a Social Security Card. There is something back here about permits and licenses.

Most of what is here may not be very interesting to read about, and may not concern you and your work now. But depending on what kind of work you do, how much money you make and where you live, some of what is here might become important. So it's probably a good idea to read it over just so you'll know a little about such things.

Some Words About Work and Money

Work is a word that has a bad name. Which is unfortunate. Because everyone needs work—not just something that is fun, and not just something that makes them rich, but something that makes them feel right at the end of each day. Some people like growing roses. Some people like making fruit pies. Some people like to knit long red scarves. Some people like to play soccer, or the mandolin. Some people like to fix cars and draw pictures. Everyone needs to do something they like. It's what tells them that they're alive. That is what work is all about.

Money is something that almost everyone would like to have lots of. It is a subject of great controversy. People write books about it, steal it, have heated arguments over it, quit their jobs over it, go on strike when they think they aren't getting enough of it. But money isn't the magic thing we try to make it. It is really just a convenient device that makes it easier for us to *trade* one thing for another. Let's say you make shoes and I grow prunes. I need a pair of shoes and you want a bushel of prunes. That's lucky, because what would you do if I didn't need shoes? You'd have to hunt all over for someone who *did*, and who happened to have something that I needed myself. And that sounds like a lot of complication. Money is not a magic thing, and it's good to remember that. There are many people who are awfully confused about that subject.

There are lots of ideas in this book for how you can play around with work and money. If you try them out on your own, then you won't have to take someone else's word for what they are all about. You'll begin to have your own ideas about what work is right for you. And you'll get some experience with that not-so-magical tool called *money*.

You and the Bank

If you earn a little money now and then, it is probably a good idea to open a savings account at a bank near you. Each bank has different rules about what they let kids do, but this is how most of them go.

If you are eighteen or over, you can do anything you want. If you are under eighteen and have no driver's license or similar identification, chances are it will be necessary for you to open a *joint savings account* with a parent or guardian. That is a polite way of saying that the bank prefers not to let kids be responsible for their own money. Your parent must sign the application card, and must sign each time you take money out. (Anyone can deposit money.) If you do have a driver's license or identification, you can probably open a savings account without an adult's signature on everything.

Some banks allow kids who are fourteen or fifteen to have their own accounts, if they are living with their parents, and especially if the bank knows the parents. Usually it's up to the bank manager. So if you are around fourteen and know what you're doing, you might be able to talk the bank manager into letting you have your own savings account if your parents have no objection.

A *checking account* is a different story. That's where you write out a check to someone and give it to them instead of cash money, and the bank pays them the money later, when they present your check. Most banks require that you be eighteen to open a checking account and have some kind of steady job. Or, that you have a *joint checking account* with an adult who must sign every check along with you *(co-sign)*. It will probably be a while before you really need a checking account anyway. But you should know what the rules are.

When you put money into a savings account, the bank pays you *interest* if you leave it there. Interest is usually paid on money that is left in the account for three months or more. How much interest is paid depends on what bank you go to. You can also put your money in a savings and loan association, which is a lot like a bank, but often pays higher interest.

You and the Government

One of the ways that both state and federal governments earn money to stay in business is by collecting taxes from people. Anyone who makes over a certain amount in any single year must pay income tax to the federal government on April 15 of the following year. Most state governments collect income taxes, too. They collect it on the same day the federal taxes are paid. (Actually, you mail it to them.)

The magic figure is $2,050. If you earn even one dollar more than that amount, in one year, you must file a tax return and pay some tax. (The magic number changes from time to time. It used to be $600.) Most kids will not earn that much money until they get regular jobs. But it's possible to earn that much, so you might as well know about income tax rules.

If you are under eighteen and living at home, you are still considered to be *dependent* on your parents no matter how much money you make yourself. So even if you make over $2,050 on your own, you must pay federal income tax, and—depending on where you live—maybe state income tax, too.

Both state and federal governments have offices in big cities. Look in the white pages under "United States Government" or the name of your state. The agency that collects federal income tax is called the *Internal Revenue Service.*

For the states, the name varies. In California it's called the *State of California Franchise Tax Board.* In your state it might be something else and you may have to ask.

There is another government agency you need to know about. It is called the *Social Security Administration.* It is the agency that pays some money every month to people when they get old enough to retire, and stop working. It functions like a big lifetime savings account. A certain portion of your income is paid into that account each time you pay income taxes. Then when you reach the age of sixty-two, you can apply to draw on that money. How much you get depends on how much money you made while you were paying into the account.

Each person who works has a card given them by the Social Security Administration which they keep all their life. It has a number on it which is how the government keeps track of that person's money. Here is what they look like:

The number at the top is the account number. And in order to file an income tax return, you'll need to have a Social Security Card like this one, with your own account number.

Anyone can apply for a Social Security Card. There is no age limit. It costs nothing. All you have to do is fill out a simple form and sign your name. You may be required to show a copy of your birth certificate when you apply, so ask your parents to keep one around in case you need it. To find out where to apply for your own Social Security Card, look in the white pages of your phone book under "United States Government" and then under "Social Security Administration." Most big cities have an office. You can get a card by mail, too.

You won't need a Social Security Card to do your own work. But you *will* need one when you get a regular job with a store or a company later on, or whenever you make enough money to file a tax return.

Keeping Track of Your Money

Even if no one asks you to do it, it's a pretty good idea to keep records. It's one way of knowing where your money is (or was). And it's the only way of knowing whether you are making money or losing it.

What we mean by keeping records is knowing how much money you have earned and how much you have spent. Because if you have to spend $5 in order to earn $3, you're not doing very well. Or rather, you're not doing very well as far as making money is concerned. You might spend $5 to put on a neighborhood circus and earn only $3 back and have so much fun doing it that you don't care about losing $2. *There is nothing wrong with that.* As long as you can afford it. And as long as you know about it. And in order to know about it, you have to keep track of your money.

There is another good reason for keeping careful records of the money you earn and spend. Friends. If you are working with friends, everyone must be very careful to be sure that each person gets a fair share of the money. And that means knowing exactly how much there is.

Here is a way to keep simple records. You can use this one or invent your own. The principle is the same no matter how you go about it.

> *money received (income)*
> *less money spent (expenses)*
> *leaves money earned (profit or loss)*

The Cigar Box Method

You'll need a cigar box (or some other small sturdy container) and a bunch of little slips of paper about 2 x 3 inches or so, some small envelopes and some rubber bands or paper clips. And a pencil.

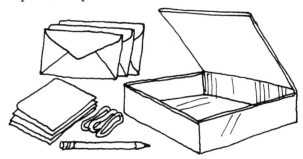

In this method, you do not use a bank to keep your money in. You use a cigar box. Which means you have to be careful. Leave it in a safe place in a drawer or cupboard.

When you spend money, you take it out of the box and write out a receipt on one of the little slips of paper. *Each time.* You can't skip even one! Each slip of paper should have this information on it: who took the money; what day; what for.

When you put money into the box, you enter the amount and the date and where the money came from on the front of one of the envelopes like this:

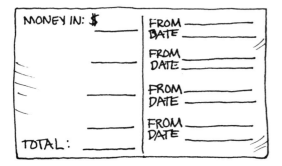

At the end of each week, or if you like, at the end of each month, you add up all the money that is written down on the front of the envelope and total it.

Then you add up all the money that is written down on the little slips of paper and deduct that from the amount on the envelope.

The difference should be equal to the amount of money that is left in the box. If there is *more* money in the box, it means that you forgot to write something on the envelope. If there is *less* money in the box, it means you forgot to fill out a little slip when you took money out. (Guess which one happens most.)

After that, you should put a paper clip or rubber band on all the little slips for the week (or month) and put them into the envelope. Then you start over again for the next week or month.

You can use the cigar box for keeping all your money and all your receipts. If your money comes from different projects, and you are spending money for ice cream cones and movies as well as for project expenses, you should keep track of each project and your own entertainment expenses separately.

Permits and Licenses

Most businesses that are run by adults are in one way or another regulated by some part of the government. Most regulation is intended to protect customers; some is intended to provide taxes which pay for running the government.

The regulation takes the form of permits or licenses (or both), and taxes. Until you are of legal age (which in most states is age eighteen), you probably won't have to think much about regulations. They are a tricky business. In most places, kids are permitted to do their work without having to bother with them.

But if you spend very much of your time doing work, and if that work brings you to the attention of local government officials who enforce regulations, you may have to think about it sooner.

If that happens, take our advice and discuss the situation with a grownup first. Chances are, whatever regulation is staring you in the face wasn't intended for kids and can be avoided. If it can't, you'll need the assistance of an adult anyway since most government agencies do not recognize the rights and abilities of kids to act for themselves in such matters.

Here are some of the kinds of permits and licenses that are the most common. Since regulations are different in different places, it is not possible to tell which of these are used where you live.

Business License. Usually issued by cities, towns or counties to anyone who takes money for things they sell. Sometimes there is a small fee for the license.

Food and Beverage License. People who sell things to eat are usually required to have a license from the Health Department. You don't need one for a lemonade stand, or for selling cookies or candy door to door. But if you do much advertising and it begins to look more like business and less like kidstuff, you might have to find out about the requirements in your area.

Sales Tax License. Regular businesses who sell anything but food usually charge sales tax, which they collect from their customers (in addition to the selling price of the item, and based on that price) and then pay to the city and the state. That's how governments make part of their money. In order to collect the tax, you must have a license and must keep very careful records of all sales.

How To Make Change

What do you do when someone gives you a dollar bill to pay for something that only costs 10 cents? Do you keep the dollar and say thanks very much? Do you give it back and say that's too much, thanks anyway? No. What you do is make change, and here's how to do it. All you have to know is how to add.

You have just sold an apple to a football fan. The apple costs 10 cents. The fan gives you a dollar bill. The football game is about to start. They are in a hurry. What do you do?

Start with the cost of the apple. Say:
"10 cents."
Then give them coins and add the coins out loud until you have added up to a dollar.

"20 cents."	(you gave him a dime)
"25 cents."	(and a nickel)
"50 cents."	(and a quarter)
"$1.00. Thank you."	(and a half dollar)

And that's it. Check and see if that's right.

        1.00 is what you got
minus .10 for the apple

        .90 change coming

A dime, a quarter, a nickel and a half dollar add up to 90 cents. Right?

Now practice with your mom or dad or anyone who can check to make sure you're correct. Do it at least ten times with different amounts until you can do it without having to go back and start over.